Spring Ayurvedic Cleanse

AYURVEDIC CLEANSE
Spring

14-Day Seasonal Cleanse to Boost Digestion, Break Bad Habits, and Feel Your Best

DR. NOAH VOLZ

SPRING AYURVEDIC CLEANSE

Copyright ©2022 Noah Volz
Published by Noah Volz and Rhythm of Healing
www.rhythmofhealing.com

All rights reserved including the right to reproduce this book or portions thereof in any form or by any means, electronic or mechanical, including photocopying, recording, or by information storage or retrieval system, without written permission of the author. All inquiries should be addressed to noah@rhythmofhealing.com.

Printed in the United States of America
First Edition

Text by Noah Volz

Photo credits
Photo on page 7 by Andrea Piacquadio
Photo on page 45 by Calum Lewis
Photo on page 81 by Tamara Gak
All recipe photos ©2021 by Noah Volz
Photo of Noah Volz ©2020 by Justin Orr Photography

Graphic Illustration credits
Cover design by 100covers
Interior design by ElfElm Publishing
Logo by Jason Harris

Disclaimer: The *Ayurvedic* information in the "Spring Ayurvedic Cleanse" is for educational purposes only. The information within the "Spring Ayurvedic Cleanse" is not intended as a substitute for the advice provided by your physician or other medical professional. If you have or suspect you have a serious health problem, promptly contact your health care provider. Always consult with a health care practitioner before using any herbal remedy or food, especially if pregnant, nursing, or if you have a medical condition.

*This book is dedicated to
my family, friends, and patients.
May it be a guide to those looking for health.*

Contents

Introduction: Who Is This Program For? 1

Part 1: Background 7
Why Me? Why *Ayurveda*? 9
Fundamentals of *Ayurveda* 19
How It All Relates: Balance 26
The Spring *Ayurvedic (Kapha)* Cleanse 36

Part 2: Preparation 45
How to Prepare 47
Dietary Recommendations 57
Herbal Guidelines 69
Lifestyle Guidelines 73

Part 3: The Cleanse 81
DAY 1-3 Preparation Phase | GOAL: Remove 83
DAY 4-7 Main Phase: Step One | GOAL: Repair 101
DAY 8-10 Main Phase: Step Two | GOAL: Restore 123
DAY 11-14 Integration Phase | GOAL: Rejuvenate 141

Part IV: Completion 159
After the Spring *Ayurvedic* Cleanse Program 161
Rasayana to Nourish the Body and Mind 162
Conclusion 168

Appendix I: Constitutional Questionnaire 171
Appendix II: Fermented Cereals and Legumes 175
Appendix III: Dry Skin Brushing - *Garshana* 178
Appendix IV: Growing Broccoli Sprouts 180
Appendix V: Fermentation - Making Your Own Kraut 184
Appendix VI: The Lymphatic System 191
Appendix VII: Stomach and HCl 195

References 199
Index 208
Recipes Index 209
Acknowledgements 210
About The Author 211

Introduction: Who Is This Program For?

Are you having trouble getting motivated in your day-to-day life? Are you resisting life changes you know will benefit you in the long run, like losing weight or getting more exercise? Do you experience:

- Excess mucous,
- Sluggish bowel movements,
- High body weight,
- Difficulty rising in the morning,
- Feeling slow, foggy, dull, lethargic, or heavy,
- Being easily attached or possessive,
- Acting overly sentimental,
- Feeling complacent or stubborn, or
- A tendency for "emotional overeating"?

In *Ayurveda* (traditional Indian medicine) these health challenges are the result of the *Kapha Dosha* which predominates in the Spring. In order to bring balance to your mind, body, and life, this program focuses on reducing *Kapha*.

This Spring Cleanse program is appropriate for most people. It is gentle, effective, and geared towards improving the function of your body and mind.

> Two things set this program apart that makes it so effective:
> **The 4 Rs and the 5 Levels.**

The Four Rs: Remove, Repair, Restore, Rejuvenate

Let's say you come into my office with back pain. I will give your back a chiropractic adjustment. This takes away the pain (Remove and Repair). Then I teach you how to safely lift heavy objects, how to improve your posture, and how to safely bend over. These new patterns are more sustainable than your old ones (Restore). Additionally, I give you some exercises to do to retrain your structure so that you have the stability and strength to prevent injury and pain in the future (Rejuvenate). This program follows that same four step process for igniting sluggish digestion, reducing attachment, and connecting you with the planet.

The Five Levels: Physical, Mental/Emotional, Spiritual, Community, Environment

Back pain is not only a physical problem. That is why you can have more pain when you are stressed. So in addition to treating your back (physical help). I will also work with you to find out how your thoughts and emotions help or hinder your recovery (mental/emotional). What beliefs you hold about your connection to spirit that may play a role (spiritual). How having or not having back pain keeps you connected with family and friends (community), and how all of that combined informs you about your sense of belonging and place in the world (environmental). The five levels are used to help remind you that health is not just physical, but requires investment in the Mental/Emotional, Spiritual, Communal, and Environmental as well. I devote an entire chapter to the 5 Levels later in the book.

Since I started leading this cleanse back in 2008, I have seen what is possible. After fourteen years, I'm confident The Spring Ayurvedic Cleanse will greatly benefit your sense of wellbeing, capacity, and joy.

My Background

When I was five years old I asked my mom how to levitate, and she told me to meditate. I sat down on the floor, closed my eyes, and waited for something magical to happen. Nothing did, so I went outside to play.

Eleven years later, at the age of 16, I browsed a flea market in Berlin when I came across a book in English called *Yoga: The Alpha and the Omega*. This book outlined instructions on how to meditate. That night, I again sat on the floor and waited for something magical to happen. It didn't happen all at once, but something did start to sprout inside me and I have been meditating ever since. Similar experiences happened with yoga and *Ayurveda*. I cannot explain the passion I felt, the insatiable appetite I grew for this knowledge.

My journey with yoga, meditation, and *Ayurveda* began to really take shape in 2002. Just after graduating from college, I traveled to Puerto Vallarta, Mexico for a yoga teacher training. After the training I decided to travel south and, after about five months, I found myself in Quetzaltenango, Guatemala. I wasn't sure what my next step was going to be, but in Quetzaltenango I re-found among my things a brochure about a yoga studio in Prescott, Arizona. On a whim I wrote the studio asking if they were hiring any yoga teachers. I received a prompt reply from Kelly—she was going to India for a year and was looking for someone to teach her classes, live in her house, and take care of her dogs. We agreed I would return to the United States so we could meet and determine if my offerings would be a good fit.

After meeting her we decided to move forward. In addition to teaching yoga, she was also an *Ayurvedic* practitioner and had an amazing library. I spent the entire year reading all her books and immersing myself fully in the wisdom of Yoga and *Ayurveda*. Both sciences have promoted more self-awareness, alignment, and physical resilience within me. I have been blessed by their depth. Therefore, from a perspective of gratitude and giving back, I seek to share these teachings in a way that is passionate, authentic, and practical. My hope is for you to experience a similar profundity of change within your life and wellbeing.

I still find myself deeply in love with the traditions that birthed yoga, meditation, and *Ayurveda*. Simultaneously, I recognize these traditions are foreign to me. Yoga, meditation, and *Ayurveda* were developed over 5,000 years ago in Asia, primarily in India and Nepal—far away from where I was born and raised, and very definitely not my own. I am a white, middle-class American; my ancestors were Welsh, Polish, and German.

It is through my middle-class upbringing I have had the privilege of being introduced to these teachings. Yoga, meditation, and *Ayurveda* were not known in the West until Westerners started visiting these places or like in the case of the British's rule of India, taking them over. It is the privilege of being born in the West that has allowed me the financial, social, and educational means to engage with these ancient sciences. Many of my teachers and mentors have been Westerners, including Dr. Mark Halpern, Dr. David Frawley, Dr. John Douillard, and Dr. Paul Dugliss. I have also studied with non-Western teachers such as Dr. Sarita Shrestha, Dr. Deepak Chopra, and Dr. Vasant Lad.

A capitalist and colonialist[1] system has allowed for the cross-cultural influence and appropriation[2] of these traditions in the West. I am only aware of a small amount of the appropriation of these traditions, and it is important for me to not contribute to this problem. It is not my intention to cause harm through the sharing of these teachings; nevertheless, it's important to note that despite my sincere intentions I am inevitably and inextricably a part of this cycle of appropriation and colonialism. So I commit to continually doing my best to educate myself and others about the greater context of the cultures from which these traditions of wisdom come.

---

1   Colonialism is the practice of acquiring full or partial control over another country's resources, people and culture by occupying and exploiting them.

2   Appropriation is the action of taking something for one's own use, without the owner's permission.

My hope is that by sharing these teachings you will grow and evolve through their wisdom, and that they will support you on your journey towards greater balance and healing. I believe this sincere approach to these traditions allows them to support the entire human family as citizens of the planet.

Contraindications

This program is designed to be safe for most people. However, certain individuals should avoid this program. Please consult with a qualified medical practitioner if you currently have—or previously have had—any of the following conditions:

- You are pregnant or are nursing,
- You are trying to conceive a child,
- You take blood thinning medications,
- You have lymphoma or cancer,
- You have Angina Pectoris,
- You have HIV or AIDS,
- You are depleted or emaciated,
- You are obese,
- You have been diagnosed with Hypertension, Congestive Heart Failure, or any heart disease,
- You currently have any type of infectious disease,
- You have undergone major surgery in the past eight weeks,
- You are highly sensitive to foods, supplements, and/or herbs,
- You have severe digestive issues such as GERD, ulcerative colitis, IBS, or celiac disease,

- You currently have Covid-19 (Corona virus) symptoms,
- You currently have a candida (yeast) infection, or
- You currently have a Herpes outbreak.

Your wellbeing matters: Thank you for being realistic in what is best for you.

Part 1: Background

Why Me? Why Ayurveda?

I grew up in an open-minded household, my parents exemplifying many of the values of the 1960s. This open-mindedness combined with travelling overseas in my teens allowed me to develop a larger worldview.

In addition, during high school in 1996, I developed an interest in cooking and a relationship with food. During my sophomore year I completed an independent study in cooking at which I worked as a dishwasher and prep cook at a local Cajun restaurant. There I developed a deep love for the art of cooking, which has continued to this day. The more I cook, the more intuitive my cooking has become. I use most recipes as a guide and rarely follow a recipe precisely. I make substitutions and additions as I go. There are, however, a few principles I often follow such as the timing of adding vegetables, how to bring out the flavors of spices, and using a mirapaux—a combination of sauteed vegetables—for soups. It is my hope and intention you will not just learn how to make the recipes in this book, but also learn how to make your cooking more intuitive as well—ultimately developing a different relationship with food. Instead of thinking of cooking as a chore to be done, creating delicious meals will become a pleasurable process for creating works of art.

In my lifetime a lot has changed in Western culture's relationship to food and nutrition. I have seen diets like the South Beach diet, Atkins diet, Whole30, Paleo diet, and now the Ketogenic diet become fads that all my patients have and are following. While every one of these diets has a lot of benefits, they often miss one key ingredient—the constitution of the person. They also imply their specific system can be used for an entire lifetime instead of being used at different life stages. We all want a silver bullet, a simple plan or system that we can use for our entire life. Unfortunately, this is unrealistic. We all go through different seasons of life. We are all different.

Ayurveda (traditional Indian medicine) recognizes bio-individuality and makes suggestions from that perspective. It also does an excellent job recognizing a teenager has different nutritional requirements than a pregnant mom or a grandmother. I created this seasonal cleanse as a reminder that your diet will change seasonally. And, that you are changing and evolving and will need to make shifts to your diet and routines to stay healthy over time.

Following these seasonal rhythms has an additional benefit of connecting you with the Earth. Humans lived in harmony with the natural world for 12,000 years before the agricultural revolution. Since then, we have been slowly domesticating animals and have developed a belief in human supremacy—which is the root of the current climate disaster. By placing ourselves above nature and using natural resources in unsustainable ways, we have been responsible for the extinction of 90% of the life on the planet. The current rate of extinction of species is estimated at 100 to 1,000 times higher than natural background extinction rates.[1,2,3] While a seasonal cleanse is not going to solve the climate crisis, it can be one additional step towards dismantling the belief in human supremacy. Participating in this cleanse can help us recognize our reliance on the natural world and to take better care of the planet within which we live.

Why do this program?

The science of medicine, and the basis of healing itself, requires we abide by the limitations of the natural world. Healing ourselves, as individuals and as a species, requires us to live sustainably and to respect all living things. This includes our bodies, and the earth from which life itself arises. In this way, traditional forms of medicine such as *Ayurveda* and the use of herbs and spices represent a revolutionary force within modern society, at odds with the Western economic model based on unending growth without repercussion and the for-profit model of modern medicine. This book will give you some tools to live in harmony with the Earth and with your own body—the goal of medicine.

In most ancient systems of medicine, the digestive tract is the key to health and healing. Digestive disorders have been around since the dawn of humans and *Ayurveda* has been helping people heal their guts for over 5,000 years.

Although we live on the same planet as our ancestors once lived, we are living in a new kind of world, one where pollution and climate change have completely changed the landscape of disease. The World Health Organization has shown that while diseases attributed to infections have decreased significantly; diseases like cancer, heart disease, and kidney failure are diseases of affluence, brought on by diet and lifestyle decisions that are correlated with higher economic status. In the last 250 years our diet and lifestyle has changed considerably to include: less exercise, air conditioning, air planes, antibiotics, artificial food color, artificial sweeteners, cars, cell phones, chronic stress, computers, electrical lightning, emulsifiers, high fructose corn syrup, genetically modified food, internet, pesticides, prescription medications, artificial preservatives, refined foods, sunscreen, synthetic chemicals, synthetic fats, television, toilets, vaccines, and much more.

We are all exposed to toxic substances in our food, air, and water which harms our bodies and the planet, such as:

- Pesticides[4]
- Plastics[5,6,7]
- Phthalates and parabens[8]
- Solvents from paints
- Hormone disruptors in city water[9]
- Internal waste that hasn't been eliminated

In *Ayurveda*, these various toxic substances are grouped under one category, called *Ama*, which means "undigested." Traditionally this word referred to overeating the wrong types of foods. In the past, *Ama* would primarily accumulate through dietary patterns that would overwhelm the digestive fire, such as overeating, eating inappropriate types of foods, or not taking enough time to eat. Although this would throw physiology out of balance, *Ama* could still be managed.

Now, in the modern era however, with pesticides, plastics, and hormone disruptors in our food and water, the term *Ama* has taken on a whole new meaning and has accumulated in new levels beyond the body's original abilities. Fortunately, we can also use the ancient knowledge of *Ayurveda* and merge it with modern science to bring around balance, healing, and longevity while living in the situations we now inhabit—even if it takes a bit more preparation, work, and sustained intention.

The Spring Ayurvedic Cleanse program has three goals:

> This book will guide you through the entire process. If you need more guidance and group support, sign up for my guided seasonal spring cleanse: www.rhythmofhealing.com/spring-cleanse.html

1. Prevent the accumulation of *Ama* (and the habits that create it) through diet, herbs, and lifestyle interventions.[10]
2. Insulate the body and mind against environmental toxins and their effects.
3. Purify the body of accumulated environmental toxins in a gentle and effective way.

Committing yourself to this seasonal Spring Ayurvedic Cleanse will allow your body's overburdened detoxification machinery to function efficiently again. Lessening the burden will lead to increased energy levels, a better overall mood, and the preservation of your health over the long term.[10,11,12]

Seasonal Cleansing

Cultures around the world celebrate spring festivals and ceremonies to welcome the light after the darkness of winter. I live in the Northern hemisphere where many pagan traditions—once used to live in harmony with the Earth—have been incorporated into the Christian calendar, such as Goundhog's Day, Valentine's Day, Mother's Day, and Easter. Most traditional cultures would also fast or give up something during the Spring. While this book does not go into the medical anthropology underlying these holidays, I will bring in elements of cleansing rituals from some of these cultures in order to amplify reverence for the birthing of new Spring life.

Through leading Spring cleanses over the past fourteen years, I have witnessed deep healing is accessed when people align themselves with these seasonal rhythms. In my experience, most cleanses are too heroic for the modern person. After having tried extreme methods like juice fasts, water fasts, supplement filled smoothies, or something more severe, I have found people end up seeking something more consistent. The Spring Ayurvedic Cleanse is just that—a gentle program meant to get you results without overdoing it. The goal is to reset your system over 14 days and to fully integrate new healthy practices into your life. The Cleanse is also meant to connect you with seasonal intelligence and the supporting *Ayurvedic* rituals.

During the two weeks of the cleanse, you will be doing things aimed at helping your body and mind eliminate *Ama*. This will also help society and the planet eliminate *Ama*, which benefits all. As mentioned earlier, the elimination of *Ama* is accomplished through the removal of certain foods, by taking herbs, and by engaging in certain lifestyle practices. Together, these practices optimize the digestive fire and gently cleanse the whole body. The cleansing response is achieved through holistic "nutrition and lifestyle modifications" rather than a one-dimensional "fad diet" approach. It will take preparation, a little extra work, and a dedicated intention, but the result will be well worth it. Additional recommendations will be provided to help you eliminate *Ama* in mind, spirit, community, and the planet.

This book is an *Ayurvedic* cookbook as well as a cleanse guide for the Spring—it merges my love of cooking and my love of *Ayurveda*. I recognize it may not be realistic for every reader to cook three different meals every day of the week. Remember, the recipes are here to help inspire you; relate with them as recommendations meant to help you stay on track.

Please note that although I use the word 'cleanse' in the title, this program is not a cleanse in the true sense of the word. True cleanses are the *Ayurvedic* detoxification practices (often called *Pancha karma*) and their Western relatives outlined in toxicology textbooks. The 'cleanse' in this book is more of a reset, an opportunity to try a new way of doing things for a couple of weeks, experience some relief, and see what new habits stick.

In the rest of this section of the book I outline my uniquely modern approach to *Ayurveda*. In part Two, I introduce the dietary guidelines and the lifestyle practices that will be with you through the entire cleanse. Part Three outlines the actual cleanse. In the Appendices, I list many resources to help you get the most out of this process.

This Spring Cleanse itself is organized into three Phases: Preparation Phase, Main Cleanse Phase, and Integration Phase. The Main Cleanse Phase is further broken down into two steps. In each Phase, there are additional recommendations that go beyond the basic diet and lifestyle practices outlined at the beginning of the book. Having led these types of cleanses since 2008, I have found that not enough time is spent on preparing for a cleanse and integrating it afterward. I will guide you step-by-step through the entire process.

I hope you learn a lot from this book. I wish you inspiration and joy, and I commend you for taking this important step towards your health and healing.

Some of the Results

Currently, it is more important than ever to give your body and the planet a break. There are a lot of great cleanse programs out there these days. This program differs from other programs because it uses the *Ayurvedic* concepts to personalize your experience. It is also different because it encompasses more than just the body, it looks at how to heal *in right relationship with the planet* by balancing the physical, mental/emotional, spiritual, societal, community, and environmental levels of your being. Here are some examples of the goals of this cleanse.

On the physical level you can expect improvement in:

- Fatigue and exhaustion[13]
- Frequent colds and flus
- Low body temperature[14]
- Difficulty losing weight[15]
- Stiff or painful joints
- Overall poor quality of life[16]

On the mental/emotional level we can expect improvements in:

- Emotional immaturity and moodiness[17]
- Brain fog[18]
- Subclinical depression and despondency

On the spiritual level you can expect improvement in:

- Amount of humility and generosity you experience
- Amount you meditate, pray, sing, or do acts of service

On the community level you can expect to:

- Develop lasting friendships
- Feel a sense of belonging and community
- Improve your ability to connect with others
- Become part of a tribe that is devoted to the evolution of consciousness

On the environmental level you can expect to:

- Connect more deeply with mountains, rivers, and trees
- Show more respect for the earth
- Feel relaxed and energized in nature

All of this is based on the principles of *Ayurveda*, which recognizes we are inextricably linked to our environment and that harmony on the inside is reflected on the outside.

In the next section I offer a generalized overview of *Ayurveda* and some specific information about *why* I encourage you to do this cleanse in particular at this time of the year. If you are familiar with *Ayurveda* and the underpinning reasons for a Kapha cleanse in the Spring, feel free to skip ahead to the next section.

Ready? Let's jump in.

History of Ayurveda

Although *Ayurvedic* concepts were first mentioned in the *Rigveda* text from the Indian subcontinent about 5,000 years ago, the medicinal practices were probably practiced long before. *Ayurveda* as it is known today is said to have begun emerging and forming during the Vedic period, between 1500–600 BCE.

During the Vedic period, people in Southeast Asia understood they were equals to plants and animals. Ailments were attributed to divine factors, and magico-spiritual means were used for treatment. Priests, as the physicians, established connections between gods and humans using plants, mantras, and other means. Local *medicinal plants were commonly spiritualized through hymns. Thereafter, the priests would administer the plant medicines at a specified place and time.* During the Vedic period the four *Vedas* (spiritual texts/books), along with their *Brahmanas* (commentaries on rituals, ceremonies and sacrifices), *Aranyakas* (text on rituals, ceremonies, sacrifices and symbolic-sacrifices), and *Upanishads* (texts discussing meditation, philosophy and spiritual knowledge), were written.[19,20]

Beginning in 600 BCE the system of Indian medicine known as *Ayurveda*—which translates to *the Science of Life*—emerged as a fully developed theory of health and disease, veering away from magico-religious thinking.

Ayurveda as we know it today is based on the medical texts *Charaka Samhita* (Charaka's collection), *Sushruta Samhita* (Sushruta's collection), and Vagbhatta's *Astangahrdaya. During this time Ayurvedic* doctors, or *Vaidyas,* laid equal emphasis on the cure of disease, prevention, and health promotion. They did this by prescribing a daily and seasonal routine and nutrition for the maintenance of a balanced state of health. The *Vaidyas* advocated harmony of body and mind, and a harmonious interaction between man and nature.[21]

While evidence-based and magico-religious medicine were once bonded together, today evidence-based medicine is now separated from magico-religious medicine. Rational medicine now has the power. This division naturally influences how medicine is administered. It is remarkable, then, that the practice of Ayurveda—and the core expression of the Vedic teachings—have been supported within Indian society for thousands of years with little interruption. Ayurveda's adherence to rational thinking for the past 2,600 years has allowed it to become a comprehensive and contemporary approach to the prevention, diagnosis, and treatment of disease.

Fundamentals of Ayurveda

In this section I will be introducing you to the five *Koshas* (sheaths), five elements, three *Doshas* (bio-energetic principles), *Agni* (digestive fire), and *Ojas* (vitality). For healing and growth to occur in this cleanse, you need a basic understanding of these concepts and how they inform your life.

Five Sheaths (*Koshas*)

As a chiropractor I have worked with many people over the years and have learned pain is not only physical. Pain takes place in the context of the person's emotions, thoughts, community, society, and planet—or the *Koshas*. While conventional medicine specializes and focuses on the physical, *Ayurveda* includes mind and spirit into the healing process. While physical methods are required for healing, they alone rarely lead to long term change. Despite being a highly empirical and rational system of healing, the goal of *Ayurveda* is the alignment of one's deepest nature and the embodiment of their unique genius. This integrative philosophy separates *Ayurveda* from conventional medicine.

The nature of Vedic sciences is to focus on the transcendant and the spiritual. A model commonly used in *Ayurveda* is called the *Pancha Maya Kosha: Pancha* translates to five; *Maya*, is interpreted as "all-pervading," "interconnected," and "interpenetrating;" and *Kosha* is traditionally defined as "traps," "entrapment," "covering," "sheaths," or "bags," because they surround or cover our true natures. So the *Pancha Maya Kosha* (also known as the five *Koshas*) roughly translates to 'the five interconnected sheaths.' The five *Koshas* have been used to remind us that we are not just minds and bodies, but that we operate on many levels.

The human system is the sum of it's many parts. While *Pancha Maya Kosha* refers to realms within the physical, I use the traditional *Koshic* model as a guide to show how human beings are interconnected with all of life, including animals and plants. Instead of looking at the five layers of a person, this book will look at the five layers of life in which humans find themselves. We are inextricably connected to the places where we live through our relationships and by recognizing our connection we can better access the eternal in life.

The Five Sheaths Used in this Book: In More Detail

I'd like to take a moment to look at each sheath in more detail, as this classification system will help explain more information later on.

1. **Physical Body** – Sometimes referred to as the 'food body' in *Ayurveda*, the physical body is dependent on your relationship with food. Do you look at food with reverence? Do you look at it as calories? Do you know where your food comes from? How you eat, what you eat, and how well you digest your food are the building blocks of the physical body.

2. **Mental/Emotional Body** – The mental/emotional body deals primarily with your sensations, intuitions, feelings, and thoughts. It can also influence your relationship with food. How do different foods make you feel? Are there specific foods you turn to when you are bored, depressed, or angry? Do these foods soothe your emotions or only act as a band-aid? Becoming aware of your dominant sensations, intuitions, thoughts, and emotions is essential in order to heal your mental/emotional body.

3. **Spiritual Body** – The spiritual body is your connection to your soul and to the deeper parts of yourself. How do you honor spirit in your life? How does spirit communicate with you? How is your diet and lifestyle influenced by spirit? It is important to explore how your lifestyle and food choices support your spiritual growth.

4. **Community Connection** – Community is how we feel a sense of belonging and meaning. Perhaps you feel a connection with a community centered around a certain way of eating.

Perhaps your community is your friends or family. How will changing your diet and lifestyle impact those closest to you? How can you ensure the changes you make will be accepted by your community and perhaps even inspire them? How does community influence the foods you eat and the ways you eat? Is your community supportive of how you want to live on the Earth?

5. **Environmental Connection** – We are all connected to the Earth on which we live. Some of us garden and hike to stay present with nature. Others of us spend very little time outdoors and live in places with very little seasonal variation. All ancient cultures have developed seasonal rituals to honor the Earth. What seasonal ceremonies do you have? How do you connect with nature? How do you modify your eating patterns based on the seasons? How do your food choices support the healing of the Earth?

Many of us in the modern world have lost this recognition and feel like we don't belong. The more you can connect to yourself, your community, and nature the more you will be supported by this underlying field of intelligence and energy. Indigenous cultures recognize the connections with their communities and land upon which they live. In many ancient cultures this connection was fostered through ritual and ceremony.

While *Ayurveda* is a ritualistic approach to health and healing, this book will focus on the rituals that fit into a modern lifestyle. In this cleanse you will reconnect with the social, communal, and environmental aspects of your being through simple recommendations that are specific to the Spring. The goal of this program is to help you move through the habitual patterns that no longer serve so you can be more open and awake, reconnecting you with your source of power and wisdom. By integrating all parts of yourself, you will be more capable to make further decisions that support health, wellness, and giving back. You will break through bad habits and poor choices so you can fully live in harmony with your true nature.

Five Elements

Five has often been considered a sacred and special number. There are five fingers, five senses, and five tastes. The five elements are one of the foundational elements of *Ayurvedic* wisdom.

I like to think of the human body as a garden. It requires the space to grow, soil to grow in, water, sun, and just the right amount of wind for pollination. The terrain of our bodies determines our health. A novice gardener may use a weed killer to help a garden grow; a master gardener will ask whether the soil has the proper minerals, adequate sunshine, and plentiful water. Were the seeds planted of high quality? Are there toxins in the soil? Like a master gardener, *Ayurveda* uses the five elements to figure out why things are happening in the body and mind. The five elements in *Ayurveda* are: Ether/Space, Air/Wind, Fire, Water, and Earth.

Element	General Qualities or Characteristics	Therapeutic effects
Ether/Space	Soft, light, subtle, smooth, associated with sound	Spaciousness, deep change
Air/Wind	Light, cold, rough, dry, subtle, associated with touch	Cellular communication, lightness, transportation
Fire	Hot, sharp, subtle, light, associated with vision	Heat, metabolism, luster, radiance
Water	Liquid, oily, cold, soft, associated with taste	Cohesiveness, softness, moisturizing, contentment
Earth	Heavy, tough, hard, dry, stable, dense, associated with smell	Grounding, centering, stability, strength, immunity

Ether/Space is the container that holds and connects things together. Even if we don't see it, we know it is there. Because we don't see or feel it, it is the lightest of the elements.

Air/Wind is often invisible to the eye but can be felt when it is in motion; Air in motions is called Wind. We can see Air on a smoggy day. We can feel Wind in our nose each time we breathe in and out, and it can be felt on our skin on a breezy day. Air is slightly denser than Space but still light.

Fire is the transformation of solids into gas states. During this transformation, energy—or heat—is created. Fire is considered light because it moves upward, but is denser than Air.

Water creates life. Every ancient culture has honored the vitality of a fresh spring where water can be collected. Because Water flows downward along the path of least resistance, it is considered heavier than Fire.

Earth is solid, mostly stable, and is non-moving. Earth is where most of our food comes from and by taking care of the soil, we take care of ourselves. In *Ayurveda,* our human bodies are often considered to be clay—the Earth element. Earth is the heaviest of the five elements.

The Three Doshas

Ayurveda combines the five elements into three *Doshas*. The individual *Doshas* and the term *'Dosha'* will be used interchangeably. The *Doshas* are the markers we use in *Ayurveda* to talk about and discern between the dynamic combinations of the elements.

Each *Dosha* plays a vital role when it comes to our physiology and anatomy. Without the functions these *Doshas* play in our physical and mental bodies, we could not be alive and conscious. Our *Doshas* govern everything in the body and provide us our individuality.

- *Vata's* space and air elements are what provide movement: of blood through blood vessels, of thoughts in the mind, of neurotransmitters between nerves. The information we take in through the five senses is processed and integrated by *Vata Dosha*. The air that we breathe (in and out) does so because of *Vata*. The empty spaces within us (lung alveoli, bone trabeculae, and—occasionally—the bladder) provide areas of transition between inner and outer. The qualities of *Vata* are light, dry, cold, and mobile.

- *Pitta's* combination of fire and water elements is what gives us the capacity to digest, metabolize, and transform (food and nutrition, learning and experiences). In the mind, *Pitta* allows us to understand what is going on around us—and provides the discernment that guides us in life. The qualities of *Pitta* are hot, oily, sharp, and liquid.

- *Kapha's* combination of water and earth elements provide our structural components (think bones, muscles, fascia). It also provides us with lubrication (your easily moving joints thank you!) and saliva (so food tastes good!). Psychologically, *Kapha* gives satisfaction and contentment. The qualities of *Kapha* are heavy, cold, slow, dense, gross, and sticky.

We each have all three *Doshas* within us; we also have varying proportions of the *Doshas*—and they manifest uniquely in each of us. Many of us have one predominant *Dosha* in our constitution: *Vata*,

Pitta, or *Kapha*. Some people have two *Doshas* that are equally predominant: *Vata-Pitta*, *Pitta-Kapha*, or *Vata-Kapha*. And some people have all three *Doshas* present in equal proportions.

It is important to note that no one object or thing can be considered purely *Vata*, *Pitta*, or *Kapha*. These are relative terms. One cannot designate a particular food, such as a carrot, as *Vata*, *Pitta*, or *Kapha* unless this classification is given context, such as how it is prepared, what other dietary articles are consumed alongside it, and the status of the person consuming it. All states of being are subject to change, and even if something could be classified as purely *Vata*, *Pitta*, or *Kapha* it cannot remain so indefinitely. Thus, in the sphere of medicine, sickness and disease occurs only when health is not actively maintained.

Ojas: Vitality

Ojas is often measured by determining a person's stamina, endurance, and vitality. If you have a lot of *Ojas*, you will find that you can work 72-hour weeks and still be energetic and present with your loved ones. You will also find you can perform well in extreme sports and challenging athletic events. Activities requiring a high level of mental and physical strength will come easily to you.

When the physical body starts to decline and injury becomes more prevalent, or the skin and hair quality diminishes, this is a sign that more *Ojas* is being used than is being produced.[26]

Agni: The Fire That Transforms

We have all heard the old maxim, "You are what you eat." In *Ayurveda*, however, this maxim is modified slightly into, "You are what you digest." The production of *Ojas* is dependent on our ability to digest, just as the building and maintenance of our bodies is dependent on what we eat. Digestion in *Ayurveda* is called *Agni*, and natural health care providers seem to agree that digestion is the key to health.

How It All Relates: Balance

We are all different. We are all individuals. Some of us have thin skin and others thick skin. Some of us have strong digestion and others have sensitive digestion. It is in knowing ourselves and then acting accordingly that we can create balance. Acting accordingly is the essence of knowing your constitution.

Nothing stays the same and so no matter what your doshic make up is, at some point your *Doshas* will go out of balance. Part of knowing your *Doshic* constitution is understanding your personal relationship with *Ojas* and *Agni*, and how working with these will help you to rebalance. Most people I see have lost a deep connection with their essential nature and make choices based on habit—habits that were helpful at the time they were formed. As humans, we grow out of things, and the habits we bring along can end up no longer supporting our health and balance, creating problems instead.

In *Ayurveda* we talk about *Prakruti*, or each person's unique expression of the *Doshas* in terms of their constitution. (This is similar to how we think of genes and DNA in Western medicine).

- Someone with a *Vata*-predominant *Prakruti* will physically and mentally express the qualities of air and ether.
- Someone with a *Pitta*-predominant *Prakruti*, on the other hand, will express the properties of fire and water.
- Someone with a *Kapha*-predominant *Prakruti* will express the characteristics of water and earth.
- Dual-*Dosha* people will express the influences of both *Dosha*'s elements
- Tridoshic people have all elements in relatively equal proportions in their *Prakruti*.

The essence of *Prakruti* aligns with your inner compass. When you are in alignment with your constitution, you can tune in to your self-knowing. You will be able to sense how a specific action will make you feel. You will be able to trust yourself to make the choices that will maintain balance in your life. *Prakruti* is self-trust.

Life Out Of Balance

In this next section I will talk about common imbalances of all the *Doshas*, and what happens to our digestion when *Agni* is out of balance.

Doshic Imbalances

Dosha	Vata	Pitta	Kapha
Elements	Space (ether) and Air	Fire and some Water	Water and Earth
Seasons	Fall until Midwinter	Spring and Summer	Midwinter until Spring
Primary Qualities	Dry, Light and Cold	Warm and Moist (oily)	Cool, Damp and Heavy
Time of Day	2:00–6:00 am	10:00–2:00 am	6:00–10:00 am
	2:00–6:00 pm	10:00–2:00 pm	6:00–10:00 pm
Time of Life	50-ish to end of life	Puberty to 50-ish	Conception to Puberty

The qualities of *Vata* are light, dry, cold, and mobile. A few possible symptoms of imbalance can be poor circulation, feeling cold, dryness of the skin and scalp, insomnia (due to the lightness and irregularity of *Vata*), osteoporosis (thinning, brittle bones), and painful arthritis (pain is *Vata*). It can also manifest as constipation and/or gas (dryness). The qualities of *Vata* are increased by consuming or being exposed to those qualities. For example, *Vata* is increased by eating raw foods (dry and cold), and cold foods and drinks. It is also increased by being exposed to extreme cold, too much activity (mobile), lack of adequate sleep, over-stimulating nocturnal activities, erratic sleeping hours, consistently staying up late, unhealthy fasting, and too much caffeine consumption. So, in order to stop *Vata* from increasing, eat warm/moist food, eat at fixed times, eat whole/grounding food, stay grounded (by practicing mindfulness), do yoga, stay warm, and sleep at the same time and for the same number of hours every night.

The qualities of *Pitta* are hot, oily, sharp, and liquid. An excess of *Pitta* can manifest as feeling hot all the time, excess or foul-smelling sweat, early balding or graying, liver malfunction (*Pitta* governs the liver), and skin issues (*Pitta* governs the skin). Some more *Pitta* related issues are ulcers, acid reflux or heartburn, inflammation, "itis" diseases, acne, and jaundice to name a few. Remember that anything hot in nature is *Pitta*. The qualities of *Pitta* are increased by eating spicy and rich food, spending too much time in the sun, doing too many goal-oriented and stressful activities, etc. Hence, in order to stop *Pitta* from increasing, eat more raw and fresh food, be more playful, cool off, and get enough sleep.

The qualities of *Kapha* are heavy, cold, slow, dense, gross, and sticky. An over-accumulation of *Kapha* leads to excess mucus, colds, obesity, depression, itching, stiff joints, and swollen glands or other forms of swelling. In the digestive system, a *Kapha* imbalance leads to a slower metabolism, feeling heavy after meals, slow and sticky stools, and bloating. In the mind, it causes laziness, depression, attachment, sadness, and grief. These qualities are increased by eating too much meat or dairy, general overeating, not exercising, obsessively buying things, and using routines for control. In order to stop *Kapha* from increasing eat less food, do new things, exercise more, and challenge yourself.

Imbalances in Agni

Imbalances in *Agni* can also increase the levels of the *Doshas*, which can in turn lead to disease. It is for this reason that the Spring Ayurvedic Cleanse program acts to bring *Agni* back into balance. *Ayurveda* has identified four primary types of digestion (*Agni*) that determine the amount of *Ojas* produced in the body.

The Four Types of *Agni*:

- **Regular and Balanced Digestion (*Samagni*):** Regular and balanced digestion is the cornerstone of good health, and leads to satisfaction, mental clarity, and emotional stability. Like all things, balanced digestion requires a combination of the right components based on the specific needs of the individual. The three areas to assess when determining balanced digestion are:

  - **Appetite:** You have few cravings, and most of them are seasonal in nature. You enjoy food but it does not rule your life. You are hungry when it is time to eat and easily enjoy two to three meals a day.

  - **Digestion:** Directly after eating and for up to four hours after doing so, you have a comfortable feeling in your body accompanied by intestinal noises that sound like a baby cooing with joy.

  - **Elimination:** You have a bowel movement at least once a day, and its consistency and shape is similar to a banana.

- **Sharp Digestion (*Tiksnagni*):** It is hot and intense and is related to excess *Pitta*. In order to reduce the hot or acidic nature of digestion, the body flushes the digestive organs with alkaline enzymatic secretions and water delivered through increased circulation. This reduces the sour or acidic nature of sharp digestion, but it also dries out the body due to the utilization of its fluids. *Ojas* is the essence of water in the body and hence this type of *Agni* depletes *Ojas*. Digestion is sharp when:

  - **Appetite:** You have excessive hunger and cravings, especially for the sweet taste as it is cooling and your body has generated a lot of heat in the form of inflammation.

- **Digestion:** You are prone to acid reflux or get a sour taste in your mouth after eating that can last up to 4 hours. Your body feels hot after eating and your heart rate increases.
- **Elimination:** Your elimination is loose and frequent. Stools are unformed or have a small circumference.

- **Slow Digestion (*MandAgni*):** It is related to an excess of *Kapha* and happens when you eat too much food. Remember how your body and mind felt after your last Thanksgiving dinner? Your digestion basically works like a fire, and slow digestion takes place when you put too many logs on the fire and they don't burn well. This leads to lots of smoke and very little heat and should automatically cause you to stop eating. The mind is powerful, however, so despite having no appetite you can still convince yourself to eat one more piece of pie. And that's when slow digestion kicks in and creates a *Kapha* imbalance. Here are some examples of slow digestion:

  - **Appetite:** Your appetite is low and you can easily survive on only 2 meals a day. But unlike balanced digestion, you tend to crave certain foods and will eat based on your cravings, not because you are really hungry.
  - **Digestion:** Because the flame of your digestion is low, you often get some gas, bloating, or a feeling of sleepiness or heaviness after eating. Over time you will be able to digest everything, but you may feel like it was a lot of work and hence need to refuel. That is why this type of digestion tends to lead to excess weight gain.
  - **Elimination:** You have at least one bowel movement a day and it is usually well-formed. However, sometimes you get the feeling that there is more in there that won't come out.

- **Irregular Digestion (*Vishamagni*):** If you are having trouble deciding whether you have sharp or slow digestion because you experience the symptoms of both, chances are that you have irregular digestion. Irregular digestion is common in individuals who are out of touch with their bodies and need to re-connect with their appetite, digestion, and elimination. This pattern of digestion leads to an increase in the *Vata Dosha* and a decrease in *Ojas*. Symptoms of irregular digestion are:

    - **Appetite:** You may have intense periods of hunger alternating with a lack of interest in food. You often eat out of boredom or may binge on your favorite foods while leaving no room for your meal. Irregular appetite often leads to grazing or snacking instead of eating true, full meals.
    - **Digestion:** Directly after eating and for up to 4 hours after doing so, you often have intestinal bloating, gas, or abdominal discomfort with lots of noises coming from your intestines.
    - **Elimination:** Your elimination fluctuates from less than once a day with dry hard stools to more than three times a day with loose stools.

All of the digestion types that are not balanced lead to the accumulation of *Ama*—the collection of toxins. *Ama* then goes on to creates traffic jams in your intestines that can lead to leaky gut and other digestive complaints.

To build a healthy *Agni* so you can live balanced in your constitution, you need to adopt a balanced approach to food that is neither overly restrictive nor hedonistic in nature. Consistent pursuit of this approach ensures your body functions in a manner that allows for a gentle and gradual normalization or even an increase in *Ojas*.

Returning to Balance

When life goes out of balance, as it will, we turn to our knowledge of our individual *Prakruti* to balance our *Doshas*.

Overactive *Dosha*	Qualities	Balancing Principles
Kapha	Cold, Wet, Heavy	Warm, Dry, Lighter
Pitta	Hot, Wet, Light	Cool, Dry, Heavier
Vata	Cold, Dry, Light	Warm, Moist, Heavier

Doshas and Sense Therapies

Remembering the power of the five senses, we can choose to use different sensations in our environments to help us balance our *Doshas*. These are the qualities you can use to balance the *Doshas* when they have accumulated in excess.

	Vata Balancing	*Pitta Balancing*	*Kapha Balancing*
Sound	Calming music and chanting, classic music, peaceful silence	Cooling, soft music, flutes, and water	Stimulating music, energizing sounds, music
Touch	Gentle and warming touch massage	Cooling soft touch/massage	Strong deep body massage
Sight	Bright, calming colors: gold, orange, blue, green, white	Cool colors: white, blue, green	Bright, stimulating colors: yellow, orange, gold, and red
Taste	Rich, nourishing food: sweet, salty, sour tastes	Sweet, bitter, and astringent	Light diet: pungent, bitter, astringent
Smell	Sweet, warm, calming, clearing: jasmine, rose, sandalwood, eucalyptus	Cool and sweet: rose, sandalwood, vetiver, jasmine	Light, warm, stimulating, penetrating: cedar, myrrh, camphor, eucalyptus

The practice of returning to balance happens while offering the opposite qualities of the *Dosha* in excess. In *Ayurveda*, **everything** is a combination of the five elements, or *Doshic* qualities, when you balance the *Doshas* you find alignment with Nature.

Time of Life, Seasons, and Time of Day

Time of Life

- The *Kapha* time of life begins from the time you are conceived and continues until puberty. This is the time of life where you grow the most; growth is *Kapha*. It is also during this time that you have a lot of colds and coughs from excess mucous, which is also *Kapha*.
- The *Pitta* time of life lasts from puberty until you retire around 65. *Pitta* symptoms of acne, ulcers, or anger are common during this time.
- After you retire, you move into the *Vata* time of life. Your hair and skin become thinner, you start forgetting things, and you get cold easily.

Seasons of the Year

- Fall is *Vata* time because it is made of the same qualities mentioned earlier. The wind blows, the air is cold, and the leaves fall off the trees. In order to balance *Vata* during this time of year we turn on the heat and wear sweaters. The *Vata* qualties are cold, mobile, dry, and light. Winter is a combination of Vata and Kapha. It is cold and wet.
- Next is the *Kapha* season of Spring. Spring is when things start growing again. *Kapha* mucous that has accumulated all winter is wanting to get out and leads to colds and sinus congestion. You can see those *Kapha* qualities in the Spring: Heavy, cold, slow, dense, gross, and sticky.

- Summer is the *Pitta* time of year because it is hot. The *Pitta* qualities are: Hot, oily, sharp, and liquid, including sweat.

I live in the Northern Hemisphere, in America, and my heritage is Northern European. At the risk of excluding others I will present the seasonal calendar from my ancestry and how it relates to the *Doshic* nature of the seasons:

Season	Date	Light and Darkness	Activity	Doshic Nature
Imbolc	Feb 1st	Turning outward toward the light	New beginnings, new life, initiation	Vata-Kapha
Spring Equinox	March 19-21	Days are longer than nights	Balance, rebirth, and growth	Kapha
Beltane	May 1	Days are longer than nights	Fertility, pleasure, joy and creativity	Kapha-Pitta
Summer Solstice	June 20-22	The longest day and shortest night of the year	Abundance, culmination of outward focused energy	Pitta
Lummus	August 1st	The sun is waning	Beginning of harvest, beginning of rest after hard work	Pitta
Autumn Equinonx	Sept. 22-24	Nights are growing longer	Ending of harvest, giving thanks	Pitta-Vata
Samhain	Oct. 31st	Turning inward toward the darkness	Remembering ancestors, magic, and mystery	Vata
Winter Solstice	Dec. 21-22	Shortest day and longest night of the year	Return of the light, hope, renewal, birth	Vata

Time of Day

The last division of nature, and how it relates with the *Doshic* constitutions, is the time of day as based on circadian rhythms.

- *Vata* dominates from 2:00 am-6:00 am and 2:00 pm-6:00 pm. *Ayurveda* believes if you get up before 6 am the lightness of *Vata* will help you rise out of bed. If you haven't managed your energy during the day then around 2 or 3 you'll need something to boost your energy. You will usually grab for something sweet because the sweet taste is related to the earth element (discussed later).

- The *Kapha* time of day is 6:00 am-10:00 am and 6:00 pm-10:00 pm. Waking up during this time can make you feel groggy because of the heaviness of *Kapha*. This is also when you arrive back from work when you often feel tired. This is a good time to either exercise or prepare for sleep. Best to get to bed by 10pm at most times of the year.

- From 10:00 pm-2:00am and 10:00 am-2:00pm is the *Pitta* time of day. That is why if you stay up past 10, you often get a second wind and have trouble getting to sleep. From 10pm until midnight your body does a liver cleanse. During the day this is the best time to have a large meal because *Pitta* is high and it governs digestion.

The Spring Ayurvedic (Kapha) Cleanse

Although modern medicine primarily focuses on physical imbalances, *Ayurveda* recognizes that true healing comes from complete balance and integration of the body, mind, and spirit.

We all want to feel a greater sense of physical, mental, emotional, and spiritual wellbeing. The modern world has lost a lot of the practices commonly used to maintain overall balance. Lifestyle practices such as lunch being the biggest meal of the day, eating seasonal foods, herbal remedies, and living with the seasons are rarely followed these days.

In the past, traditional wellness practices were included in daily routines, or as *Ayurveda* terms the *Dinacharya*. These daily routines helped promote wellness and balance. These days we follow routines and rituals that cause disease due to behaviors that stem from *Prajnaparadha,* which means misuse of the intellect or an offense against wisdom. This occurs when we see the mind, body, and spirit as separate. Although this program is primarily focused on the physical body, it works on the mind and spirit simultaneously.

In this cleanse, *Ojas* (vitality) will be supported by the lifestyle recommendations of going to bed early and balancing your daily commitments.[15] By slowing down and focusing mindfully on your experiences during the program, you will be able to replenish your stores of immunity and vitality.

Agni (digestive strength) will also be increased through the dietary recommendations that not only ensure high-quality nutrition but also give the digestive system a break. For example, sticking to three meals a day with no snacking in between allows the digestive system the time and space it needs to fully digest the previous meal before the next one arrives. The digestive system is like an assembly line, and if there is not enough time between meals, then the units on the line start to pile up and that causes *Ama*.

This cleanse is meant to reduce *Kapha*. It is best utilized during the Spring, as it is the natural time in the year when the Earth is balancing *Kapha*. In the Northern Hemisphere, plan your *Kapha* cleanse between February 1st and June 20th to be in alignment with nature and therefore, more easily able to draw support from the Earth. Spring is the natural time to find balance by warming and drying out from Winter's weather, and lightening up from Winter's darkness. We have more opportunities to move, see people, and try new things. And the natural break before plants have fully produced encourage us to eat less in quantity, which optimizes *Ojas* production by promoting peak digestive function.

Ojas is produced in healthy quantities when our digestive fire (*Agni*) is balanced, which is why the Spring Ayurvedic Cleanse program is uniquely tailored to optimize the production of *Ojas* by promoting peak digestive function. *Ojas* is like the superhero version of the *Kapha Dosha* and is the most tangible of the subtle *Doshas* because it deals with the physical form. Every tissue in the body: lymph, blood, muscle, fat, bone, and reproductive tissue has a relative strength, and when those strengths are combined, it creates your level of *Ojas*.

The *Kapha* season is a good time to practice equanimity and build your resilience. When the *Kapha Dosha* in the body is functioning properly, it creates *Ojas* which is the vitality of the body that gives you resilience, stamina, and vitality. By reducing excess *Kapha* and improving *Ojas* you will start to feel your best and be able to connect more deeply with your true nature and purpose for life on this planet.

Before we move on to the Spring Cleanse itself, let's learn a bit more about the *Kapha Dosha*—the focus of this book and an overview of the digestive process.

If you want more information on the *Vata* and *Pitta Doshas* please read one of my other books.

The *Kapha Dosha*

Kapha Dosha is made up of water and earth. This combination makes it the heaviest of the three *Doshas*. Before we go further, I recommend going outside to experience the elements of water and earth. Hold a handful of earth in your hands or take off your shoes and socks and feel the earth beneath your feet. Find a stream, river, lake, or ocean and place your hands and feet in the water.

Once you have been out in nature, start to pay more attention to the earth and water in your life. See if you can recognize the elements of water and earth in your food, friends, and environment.

- When does your body feel grounded? Which physical positions bring you a sense of stability? Can you sense inside your bones? Which of your friends are steady under stress?

- Be aware of your heartbeat and the blood circulating in your body. If you have a female body, track your monthly cycles. Be aware of how much you hydrate, and how you feel after drinking water. The next time you shower, bathe yourself slowly and acknowledge the cleansing power of water. As the water goes down the drain pray for it to find it's way to the ocean as a practice of connecting your everyday action with the Earth.

Exploring Kapha through a unique interpretation of the Five Sheaths

Kapha in the Physical

- *Kapha* controls stability in the body, lubrication (mucous), and protection (fluids lining different areas of your cavities such as joints, brain, spine, stomach, lungs, and mouth.) The main sites of *Kapha* are the joints, brain, spine, stomach,

- lungs, and mouth. *Kapha* is associated with the fat cells and lymphatic fluid, as well as the white matter of the brain and nervous system.

- When in balance in the physical body, *Kapha* manifests as dense, heavy bones, a large muscular frame, slow digestion, large eyes, thick lips, lustrous hair, supple skin, stout. *Kapha*s are heavier than other *Dosha*s.

- When the *Kapha Dosha* is out of balance in the physical body, an individual will first exhibit symptoms in the joints, brain, spine, stomach, lungs, and mouth. The body will express weight gain, congestion, respiratory issues, clammy skin, a sluggish metabolism, depression and lethargy.

- To find balance, introduce the qualities of lightness, dryness, mobility, and warmth: move, stay warm, and eat smaller portions, lighter foods. Zesty spices such as cayenne and ginger win the day.

Kapha in the Emotional/Mental

- When in balance, a *Kapha Dosha* expresses with a steady personality who is naturally content with life and can handle stress very well. The *Kapha* individual forms strong attachments, is remarkably steadfast and patient with a good memory. *Kapha* individuals are well organized, love comfort, and prefer to keep things just the way they are.

- When the *Kapha Dosha* is out of balance in the emotional/mental realms, an individual will seek out too much comfort which can lead to a lack of motivation, depression, and feeling and acting 'stuck.'

- To return to balance, seek out mental stimulation, emotional encouragement, and find your motivation.

Kapha in the Spiritual

- When in balance, a *Kapha Dosha* expresses itself as being aligned with their deeper nature and in harmony with their own compass. They are sturdy and strong in their convictions and express love, compassion, and acceptance of others. *Kapha* individuals like the structure of religious practices as these rituals help them connect more deeply with spirit.

- When the *Kapha Dosha* is out of balance in the spiritual realms, an individual will be stuck, rigid, and stubborn in their attachment to spiritual ideals. This can lead to a connection to only one small part of spirit at the exclusion of the inclusiveness and spaciousness of our spiritual nature.

- To return to balance, approach spirituality in a more physically active way—dance, hike, move. Find ways to invigorate your connection to spirit.

Kapha in the Communal

- When in balance, *Kapha* individuals in community will have many friends, and will be tolerant, devoted, grateful, considerate, peaceful, forgiving, generous, and conservative. They easily express love, appreciation, and affection, and are known for their sweet temperament. In community, *Kapha* individuals connect easily, are a stabilizing force in relationships, and have an inherent desire to help others.

- When out of balance, *Kapha* individuals will try too hard to please others. They can be greedy and overly sentimental.

- To return to balance, spend time in relationships that are supportive of your needs and leave your tank feeling full. Invest energy in yourself so you have a full cup in which to serve others.

Kapha in the Environmental

- When in balance, *Kapha* individuals have a strong connection with water and feel a deep communion with earth through the mountains, trees and rocks. They often feel a great responsibility to protect the land and they feel a deep connection and love of the land.

- When out of balance, *Kapha* individuals can get stuck in the mud. They will only focus their energy on the land that belongs to them and do not extend their vision of love beyond what they own.

- To return to balance, get outside! Run or hike on a nature trail, stand barefoot in the back yard while focusing on the Earth, plant a garden; connect with the land all around you.

Overview of the Digestive Process

In this section I merge the *Ayurvedic* knowledge presented previously with the modern scientific approach to cleansing and detoxification.

The chewing action of teeth provides a mechanical breakdown of food, which allows the chemical work to be more effective. The breakdown of food begins in the mouth with:

- amylase (the carbohydrate- and starch-digesting enzyme in saliva), and

- pH-regulating electrolytes (sodium, potassium, chloride, and bicarbonate), and saliva (lubricant).

Once enough work has taken place in the mouth, food is swallowed into the esophagus. Peristalsis, aided by gravity, physically moves the food down the esophagus and into the stomach. Within the stomach, gastrin hormone begins to coordinate the entire dance of digestion. Hydrochloric acid heats food and kills bacteria. Pepsin splits proteins into smaller amino acid molecules, and mucus protects the stomach lining.

Remember this is not a true cleanse in the sense of the word and is really meant to be a way to reset your lifestyle, in order to support your practices of healthier habits on a regular basis.

From the *Ayurvedic* perspective, this first stage of digestion is the *Kapha* stage. It spans the time from first noticing a feeling of hunger (ie: from 10–15 minutes before eating) until 30 minutes after the last bite. *Kapha Dosha* is mainly responsible for the necessary protection of the mouth, esophagus, and stomach from the strong acids associated with the *Pitta* digestive enzymes of hydrochloric acid and pepsin. *Kapha* also accounts for the alkaline enzymes, such as amylase, which digest carbohydrates. When carbohydrate digestion is compromised, it is often an indication of impure *Kapha* at this stage of digestion. Another possibility is the overproduction of *Kapha*, which leads to excessive mucus and sleepiness after eating.

The primary function of the small intestines is to further break down and absorb the sugar, amino acids, fatty acids, and nutrients that have already been broken down in the mouth and stomach. The nutrients are absorbed through the lining of the small intestine and move directly into circulation.

The small intestine is divided into different sections based on localized functions. The first part is the duodenum; known as the first part of the small intestine, it is really a continuation of the lower stomach. The gall bladder and pancreas both secrete their enzymes into the duodenum. The duodenum also secretes bicarbonate, which neutralizes stomach acids.

In the jejunum, the second section of the small intestine, trypsin and chymotrypsin split proteins into polypeptides, which is then split into individual amino acids by the enzyme, peptidase.

The final section of the small intestine, the ileum, primarily absorbs vitamin B12 and bile acids as well as any remaining nutrients.

Overall, the small intestine is an acidic environment, so this is a *Pitta* zone of digestion. This acidity is buffered by pancreatic secretions before they cause damage to the inner lining of the intestine. If *Pitta* is too high, the acids might burn the intestinal mucosal lining, leading to symptoms such as belching, heartburn, hyperacidity, foul-smelling gas, indigestion, and loose stools.

The residue of indigestible material continues through the small intestine and moves into the large intestine, also known as the colon, along with the addition of spent red blood cells, spent white blood cells, spent bile salts, and mucus. These substances are processed by the large number of bacteria present in the colon in preparation for excretion. Excess water is reabsorbed in the large intestine, and bacteria feed on fiber to produce niacin (B3, B5), folic acid, Vitamin K, B12, and short-chain fatty acids. Due to its action of drying out fecal matter, the colon is considered the *Vata* aspect of the digestive process. This stage lasts 90 minutes to four hours after eating.

The pancreas is a *Pitta* organ with secondary *Kapha* undertones. The pancreatic enzyme lipase breaks down fat, and a host of other enzymes (such as cholecystokinin, gastric inhibitory peptide, etc.) break down starches. These enzymes are part of the pancreas's exocrine function. In addition to exocrine function, the pancreas also has endocrine functions—meaning some chemicals move directly into the blood stream. The endocrine functions relate to blood-sugar regulation through glucagon and insulin. The hormone insulin is used to break down glucose, or blood sugar, to transport glucose into cells and to transport amino acids. Glucagon creates more sugar in the blood which is to be stored in the liver as glycogen. The storage of glycogen in fat tissues is a *Kapha* function, where all the other functions of the pancreas are *Pitta* functions.

Bile is synthesized by the liver, and then passed to the attached gall bladder, where it is stored. From there, bile is secreted into the duodenum of the small intestine. The bile salts secreted by the gall bladder break fats into triglycerides. These are reabsorbed in the colon to be reused. When the liver is overtaxed, cholesterol and other metabolites will overflow into the gall bladder, thickening the bile, and eventually leading to gallstones. The gall bladder is classified as a *Pitta* organ.

To learn more about digestion visit Appendix VII.

Although the liver is not directly a part of the GI tract, it is a very important organ in the digestive process, and it relates to the *Pitta* and *Kapha Doshas*. When wastes are present in the blood, the liver converts them into substances that can be safely eliminated from the body. The liver also works in conjunction with the thyroid gland to regulate heat and other metabolic processes. As *Kapha* governs structure, any function of the liver that synthesizes something relates to *Kapha*, and any metabolic processes relate to *Pitta*.

Conclusion to Part 1

In Part I you learned the history and basics to *Ayurveda*—including the Five Sheaths, Five Elements, Three *Doshas*, *Ojas*, and *Agni*. You learned about how the *Doshas*, *Koshas*, and Elements work together to create *Prakruti*, or an individual's constitution. You learned what happens when things go out of balance, and some ways to bring them back into balance, specifically through the benefits of seasonal cleansing. You also learned the basics behind this Spring Cleanse, including in-depth information about the *Kapha Dosha* shared through the lens of the *Koshas*, and the science of digestion and how that relates to the *Doshas*.

It bears emphasizing—*when we are in balance, these bio-energetic principles attract us to the foods and lifestyle practices that will continue to maintain balance.* With this information, you are ready to move forward into preparing for a successful Spring cleanse.

One last note: The *Doshas* are familiar concepts to many in the world of yoga and wellness and help provide solutions specific to the individual. Because this book is not a personalized program, it can be challenging to provide customized solutions. This book instead focuses on a general *Kapha* balancing diet and a lifestyle promoting an improvement in the functions of *Agni* and *Ojas* and the elimination of *Ama*. If you are interested in a personalized program, please email me at noah@rhythmofhealing.com and inquire out my Individualized Cleanse options.

Part 2: Preparation

How to Prepare for a Successful Spring Ayurvedic Cleanse

In part Two of this book, you will learn:

1. Setting intentions
2. Building long-term habits
3. More about the four R's and how they will be used in conjunction with the five levels
4. *Ayurvedic* nutrition
5. The dietary recommendations used for the duration of the cleanse, including information about appliances to use and brands to buy
6. Herbal recommendations
7. Lifestyle guidelines
8. Additional preparation suggestions, such as how to get support from family and friends, teas, and an overview of the importance of water

At the end of part Two, I offer a preview of the upcoming cleanse.

Setting Intentions

As mentioned earlier, the goal of this cleanse is to achieve more health and vitality using the principles and practices of *Ayurveda*. If you have done a cleanse before, you know the somewhat impersonal goal of "general health" may not provide enough motivation and inspiration to keep you going when the cleanse gets difficult. It is important to remember that health is not a goal by itself, but instead a means to an end.

To be able to get through the whole program, it is important to find a deeply personal reason to do it. Perhaps you have kids and you want to stay healthy and energetic so you can spend a long, fully involved life with them. Perhaps your health challenges are stopping you from doing things that you love, or maybe you have a family history of disease. Perhaps you meditate daily and you know a clean body will help you spiritually connect better with your deeper essence. Find the reason that is right for you and strong enough to keep you going. Then write it down and revisit it whenever things get challenging.

Building Long-Term Habits

The Spring Ayurvedic Cleanse program is meant to be simple and effective. If you feel like the program is too heroic, then you may need to modify it. One of the objectives of this program is to interrupt the pattern of your life just enough to create a window of opportunity for change. When you have completed the cleanse, it is unlikely you will continue to do everything outlined in this book. So it is important to take stock of the recommendations you really enjoyed. Maybe it was a physical lifestyle practice, or maybe it was deciding to do everything with more awareness. Commit to implementing that one practice and be consistent with it. In time, that practice will automatically build upon itself.

While doing this cleanse, keep in mind that building long-term habits takes top priority. Through the studies of neuroplasticity we know the more we do something the better we get at doing it. So remember this cleanse is less about getting it right and more about practicing the new habit often. The practice may involve something as simple as trying new recipes so you have new dishes in your repertoire.

Further, it is important to always be kind to yourself when you've had setbacks, and to adopt a general approach of positivity. As you go through this program, notice the thought patterns associated with your new habits. Are you feeling good while learning those new recipes? Or is it feeling like a chore, hence draining your energy? *Always practice things you want to get better at—not just from a physical perspective but a mental perspective as well.* Habits built in a forceful manner using negative motivation usually don't last in the long term. Build new habits in a gentle and mindful way.

The Four R's

In the last section I shared that *Kapha* accumulates in the Winter and can be removed in the Spring. It is removed by increasing digestive fire (*Agni*) and removing toxins (*Ama*). This leads to an increase in vitality (*Ojas*).

In *Ayurveda* digestion is not a process that solely takes place in the digestive system. The process also takes place on the mental/emotional, spiritual, communal, and environmental levels. *Ayurveda* recognizes true health and wellness require balance in every aspect of our lives. Everything is connected. Many people think of improving physical digestion when they think of a cleanse; this program focuses on improving your function in all five of the previously described levels.

The four phases of this cleanse are remove, replace, restore, and rejuvenate. At each phase recommendations for all five levels will be made. Here are some of the results that you can expect in each phase:

Remove

This is the first phase of the cleanse, and your attention is being directed to transitioning from habitual patterns of eating and living into more conscious patterns. The removal phase is all about requiring you to clear things from your diet and life that are no longer serving you— so you can ignite your *Agni* to remove *Ama*.

PHYSICAL

- Remove Ama producing foods and stimulate the release of hydrochloric acid (HCl). Sufficient stomach HCl helps:
- Prevent the development of leaky gut by breaking down food proteins into smaller amino acids.
    - Sterilize the small intestine to help prevent the overgrowth of bacteria.

- Prevent food poisoning and parasites from gaining a foothold in your digestive tract.
- Stimulate the gallbladder to secrete bile to break down fats.
- Stimulate the pancreas to secrete digestive enzymes.

MENTAL/EMOTIONAL

- Remove unhelpful habitual ways of thinking, including how you think about your emotions.
- Remove emotions such as depression, greed, and lethargy.
- Recognize the connections between the foods you eat and your mental health.
- Recognize how you manage your emotions with food.

SPIRITUAL

- Remove busyness that takes away the time and motivation for spiritual practices such as prayer and meditation.
- Remove distracting habits and routines getting in the way of pursuits connecting you to your spiritual nature.
- Remove things in your life that don't help you connect with your spiritual nature.

COMMUNITY

- Remove rituals and practices keeping you lonely and making you feel disconnected from others.
- Remove the fears that create social anxiety.
- Remove thoughts that allow you to see yourself as separate from other people.

ENVIRONMENT

- Remove planet-harming practices.
- Remove plastic packaging from your life.
- Remove packaged food as this creates waste that goes into landfills.

Repair

In the second phase of the cleanse, you will turn your attention to repairing *Agni*, so you can digest the experiences in your life more fully.

PHYSICAL

- Repair healthy HCl production.
- Repair small intestine, pancreas, and gallbladder functions.

  ➢ When food enters the small intestine, the pancreas secretes digestive enzymes to help digest sugars, fats, proteins, and starches. Many food intolerances are linked to insufficient pancreatic enzyme output. The more thoroughly the gut digests foods, the less likely your immune system is to react to them.

MENTAL/EMOTIONAL

- Repair thoughts and emotions so they support long-term health.
- Repair the relationship with self and experience more self-love.
- Repair your relationship with food so your thoughts can support all other levels.

SPIRITUAL

- Repair the relationship with your deeper nature.
- Repair the parts of your life that make it difficult to make time for spiritual practice.
- Repair your ability to have an open heart.

COMMUNITY

- Heal your relationships with everyone in your life.
- Repair any strained community connections.
- Repair your love and trust of community.

ENVIRONMENT

- Repair your relationship with the planets soil, water, and trees.
- Repair your relationship with rituals that protect and nurture the planet.
- Repair how you view yourself as connected to the planet and its health.

Restore

In the third phase of the cleanse your attention is guided to restoration of the natural strength and resiliency of the body and digestive tract.

PHYSICAL

- Restore physical health through calorie restriction.
- Restore longevity and gut health.
- Restore the digestive tract.

MENTAL/EMOTIONAL

- Restore a positive self-image.
- Restore self-love and self-respect.
- Restore healthy self-esteem and confidence.

SPIRITUAL

- Restore the practices and routines that connect you with your inner nature.
- Restore daily routines of prayer and presence.

COMMUNITY

- Restore a sense of community and belonging.
- Restore the practices that connect you with community.
- Restore a sense of interconnectedness.

ENVIRONMENT

- Restore a lifestyle that protects the planet.
- Restore your relationship to the planet and its seasonal rhythms.
- Restore your love of the planet and work for its protection.

Rejuvenate

In the fourth phase your attention is directed to daily practices that allow you to rejuvenate your health and energy.

PHYSICAL

- Rejuvenate your microbiome.
- Rejuvenate your immune function.
- Rejuvenate your digestive strength.

MENTAL/EMOTIONAL

- Rejuvenate your mental and emotional resilience.
- Rejuvenate your ability to express love and compassion.
- Rejuvenate your self-trust and generosity.

SPIRITUAL

- Rejuvenate the rituals and routines that connect you with your soul.
- Rejuvenate all the positive qualities of your soul.
- Rejuvenate your connection to life, love, and happiness.

COMMUNITY

- Rejuvenate the relationships that help you build community.
- Rejuvenate your connection to community.
- Rejuvenate social circles that feed your joy.

ENVIRONMENT

- Rejuvenate the environment and, therefore, the planet through your choices.
- Rejuvenate your local environment.

Each phase of the cleanse offers specific recommendations in order to accomplish the goals of the Four R's. In addition to these more specific recommendations, general guidelines are also offered in order to give you the strong foundation for healing. These include dietary, herbal, and lifestyle recommendations. These will be covered in detail next.

Ayurvedic Nutrition

The core of this program revolves around food. The recipes are based off a diet that is seasonal, *Kapha* reducing, *Agni* enhancing, and free of common food allergies.

Ayurvedic nutrition is based on the six tastes. Like the *doshas*, the six tastes—or *Rasas*—are composed of the elements in order to describe how certain foods affect the body. The six tastes, their energies, examples of foods, organs, and which *Dosha* they increase are outlined in the table below:

Rasa	Energy	Foods	Organs	Increase
Sweet	Cold	Sugar, Grains	Spleen/Pancreas	*Kapha*
Sour	Acidic/hot	Kombucha, Wine, Pickles	Liver	*Pitta*
Salty	Hot	Table Salt, Seaweed	Kidneys	*Kapha* and *Pitta*
Pungent	Hot	Hot Peppers, Wine	Lungs	*Pitta*
Bitter	Cold	Burdock root, Dandelion greens	Heart	*Vata*
Astringent	Cold	Black Tea, Beet Greens	Colon	*Vata*

In order to reduce Kapha and increase Agni, follow these recommendations:

Best Qualities: Hot, dry, light

Qualities to Avoid: Cold, wet, heavy

Best Taste: Pungent, bitter, astringent

Tastes to Avoid: Sweet, sour, salty

Seasonal eating

Many of the foods that reduce *Kapha* are ready to eat in the spring. Although it is not required for this cleanse, I highly recommend you develop a relationship with where your food comes from. That may mean developing a relationship with the farmer from whom you buy at the market, or the produce person at the natural food store where you shop. Knowing the people who grow or distribute your food connects you with the planet. Eventually you may feel inspired to grow most of your food yourself—another small step towards living on the earth with respect. *Ayurveda* recognizes how interconnected all of life is and that individual health relies on living on a healthy planet.

Dietary Recommendations for the Spring (Kapha) Season

The dietary recommendations are based on three elements:

1. Food that comes ripe in the spring, or between February and June. I live on the West coast, so I have based many of the food recommendations on what is in season here. If you want more information for seasonal foods in your area, please use www.seasonalfoodguide.org.
2. Following an elimination diet in which you restrain from eating meat, dairy, gluten, soy, corn, caffeine, and refined sugar.
3. Eat foods that improve *Agni* in order to remove the sluggish digestion caused by excess *Kapha* in the body.

This list is broken up into three categories: green light, yellow light, and red light. The green light section lists the foods, fats, herbs, and spices that will make up the bulk of your diet during the Spring Ayurvedic Cleanse. The yellow light section is the foods that should only be consumed in small amounts. The red light section highlights foods to be avoided during this time.

Integrating these three factors creates a food list that is both seasonal, ignites Agni, and eliminates common food allergens.

Green Light: Prioritize these Foods

VEGETABLES (PREFERABLY COOKED, LOCAL, AND ORGANIC)[22,23,24,25]

FEBRUARY

- ❏ Apples
- ❏ Chard
- ❏ Fennel
- ❏ Garlic
- ❏ Kale
- ❏ Leeks
- ❏ Mushrooms
- ❏ Onions
- ❏ Potato
- ❏ Rapini
- ❏ Rutabaga
- ❏ Sprouts
- ❏ Winter squash

MARCH

- ❏ Chives
- ❏ Green onion
- ❏ Leeks
- ❏ Nettles
- ❏ Rhubarb

APRIL

- ❏ Asparagus
- ❏ Fiddleheads
- ❏ Tarragon
- ❏ Thyme

MAY

- ☐ Arugula
- ☐ Cauliflower
- ☐ Cilantro
- ☐ Collards
- ☐ Endive
- ☐ Fava beans
- ☐ Lettuce
- ☐ Mint
- ☐ Mustard greens
- ☐ Nettles
- ☐ Oregano
- ☐ Parsley
- ☐ Pea shoots
- ☐ Purslane
- ☐ Radicchio
- ☐ Radish
- ☐ Rosemary
- ☐ Sage
- ☐ Sorrel
- ☐ Spinach
- ☐ Watercress
- ☐ Broccoli sprouts (Spring)
- ☐ Burdock
- ☐ Celeriac
- ☐ Celery

FRUITS

- ☐ Lemon
- ☐ Strawberry

SEEDS (AND THEIR BUTTERS AND MILKS)—TRY SPROUTED OR SOAKED

- ☐ Chia
- ☐ Flax
- ☐ Pumpkin
- ☐ Sesame
- ☐ Sunflower
- ☐ Hemp

BEANS/LEGUMES (SOAKED AND PRESSURE COOKED)[26]

- ❑ Aduki
- ❑ Black
- ❑ Lentils
- ❑ Mung
- ❑ Pinto
- ❑ Red

FATS/OILS[27,28]

- ❑ Extra virgin sesame oil: low-medium heat, 350F/175C
- ❑ Extra virgin coconut oil (not copra): low medium heat, 350F/175C
- ❑ Extra virgin olive oil: medium heat, 405F/210C
- ❑ Extra virgin almond oil: medium heat, 420F/216C
- ❑ Organic grass-fed cultured ghee: high heat, 485F/252C

RAW, UNPASTEURIZED FERMENTED FOODS[29]

- ❑ Krauts
- ❑ Kimchee
- ❑ Pickles
- ❑ Coconut kefir
- ❑ Apple cider vinegar

SEA SALT WITH HIGH MINERAL CONTENT

- ❑ Celtic
- ❑ Himalayan
- ❑ Hawaiian Re

HERBS AND SPICES[30]

- ☐ Mustard
- ☐ Ginger
- ☐ Garlic
- ☐ Cilantro
- ☐ Cumin
- ☐ Coriander
- ☐ Fennel
- ☐ Cinnamon
- ☐ Nutmeg
- ☐ Cardamom
- ☐ Turmeric
- ☐ Fenugreek
- ☐ Chili powder
- ☐ Curry powder
- ☐ Italian seasoning
- ☐ Basil
- ☐ Rosemary
- ☐ Tarragon
- ☐ Oregano

- Eat as many mustard greens, seeds, and condiments as possible.
- Eat as much cooked red cabbage as possible.
- And, lastly, include broccoli sprouts in as many meals as possible.

Yellow Light: Only Eat Small Amounts of These Foods

- ☐ Carrots
- ☐ Eggplant
- ☐ Potatoes (white or red)
- ☐ Tomatoes
- ☐ Raw honey
- ☐ Miso
- ☐ Tempeh
- ☐ Apples
- ☐ Dried cranberries (if fruit-sweetened)
- ☐ Pear
- ☐ Coconut milk, butter, oil

Red Light: Avoid These Foods

- ☐ All food additives and artificial sweeteners[31]
- ☐ All processed or packaged foods[32]
- ☐ All fried foods and trans fats[33]
- ☐ Animal protein (broths made from bones are fine)
- ☐ Coffee
- ☐ Dairy (except for cultured ghee)
- ☐ Sugar and all commercial sweeteners
- ☐ Soy (except fermented soy: miso, Tamari, and tempeh in small amounts)
- ☐ Glutinous grains, including wheat, spelt, kamut, rye, oats, barley[34,35,36]
- ☐ Processed sugars and sweeteners
- ☐ Caffeine in all forms including chocolate (matcha green tea is okay in moderation)
- ☐ Most non-organic foods

Follow an Elimination Diet

During the entire cleanse you will be following an elimination diet. This is a diet eliminating all the red light foods. To recap, these are: sugar, alcohol, caffeine, chocolate, soy, wheat/gluten, meat, dairy (except cultured ghee), too many nuts, and corn. These foods are avoided because many are common food allergies. You may also choose to reduce the amount of boxed, canned, and packaged foods as well, because many of them contain unhealthy preservatives. Focus on eating whole foods that are organic, seasonal, colorful, and fermented. If in doubt, shop at your local farmer's market, or shop around the edges of your co-op or grocery store.

General Principles

Proper diet and routine will balance the *Dosha*s. The three general principles found in the *Vedic* texts are: how, when, and what to eat.

Here are the rules for how and when to eat to reduce *Kapha* in this Spring Cleanse:

How to Eat

- Wash your hands prior to eating.
- Set a specific time and place for your meals. Be consistent and don't eat late at night.
- Create a pleasant eating environment. No distractions.
- Bless your food before eating.
- Eat with a calm mind. Don't rush.
- Take your time and chew your food longer as it allows digestion to begin in the mouth. And remember that mindfully enjoying the taste of food in your mouth reduces the amount of food you end up eating.
- Eat until you are 75% full. You need at least 25% space for good digestion to take place.
- Eat only after your previous meal is fully digested (three to six hours).

When to Eat

- Stick to three meals a day and do not snack in between meals. If you are working with *Kapha*, then two meals a day is even better than three. If you absolutely need to eat something, have fruit.
- Most people with excess *Kapha* eat too frequently. If you are not used to eating two to three meals a day, start with four or five, and work your way down to two or three a day.

What to Eat—Stock Your Pantry Shopping List

Many of the recipes in this manual require you to have some common pantry items. Although this list is not exclusive to this program, it will give you a sense of some common supplies you may need to have available if you want to reduce *Kapha* in your diet. It is likely you will already have many of these.

GRAINS

- ☐ Millet
- ☐ Quinoa
- ☐ Wild rice
- ☐ Tapioca flour

BEANS

- ☐ Split mung beans
- ☐ Black beans

NUTS AND SEEDS

- ☐ Flaxseeds
- ☐ Tahini

OILS

- ☐ Organic unrefined sesame oil
- ☐ Organic virgin coconut oil
- ☐ Extra virgin olive oil
- ☐ Organic grass-fed cultured ghee

CONDIMENTS AND OTHER

- ☐ Dijon mustard
- ☐ Balsamic vinegar
- ☐ Apple cider vinegar

HERBS AND SPICES

- ☐ Salt
- ☐ Garlic cloves
- ☐ Ginger powder
- ☐ Cumin powder
- ☐ Clove powder
- ☐ Fenugreek seeds
- ☐ Mustard seeds
- ☐ Coriander powder
- ☐ Fennel powder
- ☐ Cinnamon powder
- ☐ Nutmeg powder
- ☐ Cardamom powder
- ☐ Fenugreek powder
- ☐ Chili powder
- ☐ Curry powder
- ☐ Garam Masala
- ☐ Asafoetida (Hing)
- ☐ Italian seasoning
- ☐ Basil, dried
- ☐ Rosemary
- ☐ Oregano
- ☐ Nutritional yeast

SWEETENERS

- ☐ Stevia

FRUIT

- ☐ Lemon
- ☐ Lime

VEGETABLES

- ☐ Broccoli seeds

Recommended Appliances

- **Thermos flask:** You are going to be drinking a lot of tea, so it is good to have a large thermos flask—at least 40 ounces/1.2 liters—to keep your beverages warm. I also like to have a smaller thermos I can use to take warm food, like soups, with me on the go. This is a great option for a lunch when you are away from home.

- **Pressure cooker:** During the program, it is recommended you cook all your beans and lentils in a pressure cooker. I recommend an electric pressure cooker like the InstaPot (Instant Pot). A pressure cooker is a sealed pot that uses both heat and high pressure to reduce your cooking time. In addition to this, it can neutralize many of the antinutrient factors in legumes.[39,40] A quick Google search will show you how long it takes to cook beans in a pressure cooker but, in general, most beans take 30 minutes and most lentils take 15 minutes.

Recommended Brands

As you move towards a relationship-based system of food consumption—one in which you are aware of your buying decisions and how they impact your health as well as the health of the planet—it is important to minimize buying packaged products. Instead support local farmers. When this is not possible, make sure you choose brands that have a commitment to sustainable practices. Many big-name brands are natural and organic, but they rarely have practices that are good for the planet. Find brands you want to support and with which you would like to build a relationship. Here are some of the brands I currently support because of their practices. Chances are you will find local brands that you can support as well.

Food Grade Oils

- **Barlean's Organic Oils** www.barleans.com
- **Omega Nutrition Oils** www.omeganutrition.com
- **Nutiva Oils** www.nutiva.com
- **Spectrum Oil** www.spectrumorganics.com
- **Pure Indian Food (for their cultured ghee)** www.pureindianfoods.com

Herbs and Spices

- **Banyan Botanicals** www.banyanbotanicals.com
- **Mountain Rose Herbs** www.mountainroseherbs.com
- **Oshala Herbs** www.oshalafarm.com

In the Kitchen

When purchasing kitchen appliances, buy used appliances whenever possible to cut down on packaging waste. If you are buying a new appliance, buy something that will last for a long time or has a lifetime warranty. Also consider the brand's energy star rating. At the time of this writing, I could not find any brands that were specifically devoted to environmentally friendly practices, so I have listed the brands I like and use.

For more suggestions check out clarifygreen.com/sustainable-kitchen-appliances/

- **Vitamix high speed blender** www.Vitamix.com
- **Vitaclay nontoxic ceramic cookware** www.vitaclaychef.com
- **Cuisinart** www.cuisinart.com
- **InstaPot pressure cooker** www.instantpot.com

Teas

A recent study showed that one plastic tea bag can shed one billion microplastic particles into your drink.[41] Here is a list of tea bags that do not contain micro plastics.

- **Yogi Teas** www.yogitea.com
- **Organic India Tulsi Teas** www.organicindiausa.com
- **Traditional Medicinals** www.traditionalmedicinals.com
- **Pukka Teas** www.pukkaherbs.com

Herbal Guidelines for the Spring Ayurvedic Cleanse

Auyrveda's beauty lies in its ability to customize recommendations to the individual. I look at the unique characteristics of a client's symptoms and develop an herbal formula specifically balancing their experiences. Because this specificity is not possible in this format, I have developed a two-level approach for the herbal formulas.

The first level involves using herbs that are both gentle and effective. The second level is going to be stronger and more therapeutic. (You could also attain the second level's effects by doubling the dose of the herbs that you are taking in the first level.)

Which path you choose depends on you.

- If you consider yourself sensitive, or if you have never done this cleanse before, choose Level 1.
- If you have done the cleanse before and it went well, choose Level 2.

Remember: The level you choose does not reflect how "strong" or "heroic" you can be—this cleanse is designed to meet you realistically where you are, moving you a step forward, and developing healthy new long-term habits.

Level 1 Herbal Recommendations (Duration: 2 Weeks)

You can purchase these herbs, supplements, and oils individually using the links above, or you can purchase an all-inclusive Level 1 kit at www.rhythmofhealing.com/store/p45/Spring_Product_Kit_-_Banyan_Botanicals.html

Before Meals

Take these herbs with a few sips of water before meals:

- Banyan Botanicals Sweet Ease:[42,43] Take 1 tablet, 3x/day, before meals.
    - www.banyanbotanicals.com/sweet-ease-tablets-10/

- *Kapha* Digest:[45] Take 1 tablet, 3x/day, before meals.
    - www.banyanbotanicals.com/Kapha-digest-tablets-10/

After Meals

Take these herbs with a few sips of water up to 15 minutes after meals:

- Banyan Botanicals Total Body Cleanse:[45] Take 1 tablet, 3x/day, after meals.
    - www.banyanbotanicals.com/total-body-cleanse-tablets/

- Banyan Botanicals Blood Cleanse Tablets: Take 1 tablet 3x/day, after meals.
    - www.banyanbotanicals.com/blood-cleanse-tablets-10/

Before Bed

Take these herbs before bed with a few sips of water:

- Banyan Botanicals Triphala Tablets:[46] Take 2 tablets each evening.
    - www.banyanbotanicals.com/triphala-tablets-11/

- Banyan Botanical Tranquil Mind:[47] Take 2 tablets each evening.
    - www.banyanbotanicals.com/shop/health-topic/sleep/tranquil-mind-tablets-10/

- *Kapha* Massage Oil:
    - www.banyanbotanicals.com/Kapha-massage-oil/

Level 2 Herbal Recommendations (Duration: 2 Weeks)

You can purchase these herbs, supplements, and oils individually using the links provided or you can purchase an all-inclusive Level 3 kit at www.rhythmofhealing.com/store/p47/Spring_Product_Kit_-_Kottakkal.htm

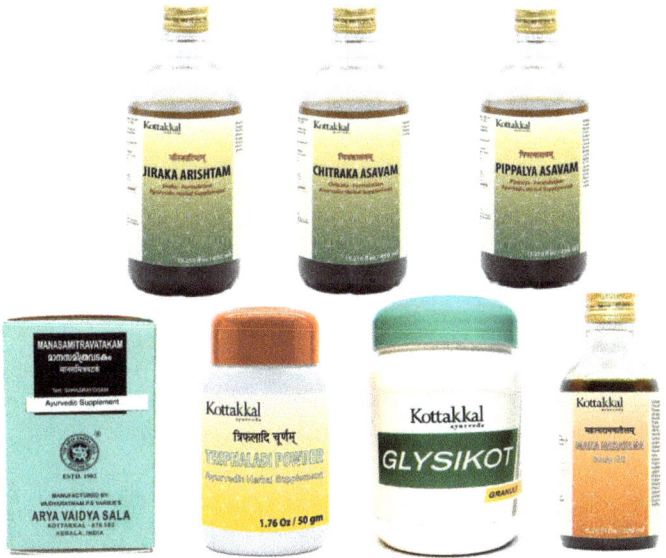

Before Meals

Take these herbs with a few sips of water 15 minutes before meals (or right before):

- Kottakkal Glysikot Granule: Place ½–1 Tablespoon of granules in 2–4 ounces of water. Do this before meals.
    - www.kottakkal.shop/collections/health-support/products/glysikot-granule

- Chitraka Asavam: Place 1–1 ½ Tablespoon of asavam in water and take before meals.
    - www.kottakkal.shop/collections/arishtas-asavas/products/chitraka-asavam

After Meals

Take these liquids after meals.

- Pippalya Asavam: Place 1–1 ½ Tablespoon of asavam in water and take before meals.
    - www.kottakkal.shop/products/pippalya-asavam

- Jiraka Arishtam: Place 1–1 ½ Tablespoon of arishtam in water and take before meals.
    - www.kottakkal.shop/products/jiraka-arishtam

Before Bed

Take these herbs before bed with 4 ounces of water.

- **Kottakkal Triphaladi Churnam:** Place 1-2 teaspoons of powder in water and take in the evening.
    - www.kottakkal.shop/products/triphaladi-churnam

- **Kottakkal Manasamitra *Vatakam*:** [55,56] Take 2 tablets each evening.
    - www.kottakkal.shop/products/manasamitra-Vatakam

ADDITIONAL SUPPLIES

- **Maha Narayan oil:**
    - www.kottakkal.shop/products/maha-narayana-oil

> **Please note:** Your herbal bottles will not be empty after the two-week cleanse. You can safely keep taking these herbs until the bottles are empty, and if there is a formula you really liked and benefitted from, you can continue taking it on a long-term basis by purchasing more online.

Lifestyle Guidelines for the Spring Ayurvedic Cleanse

Ayurveda adapts and changes with the seasons; many of *Ayurveda*'s general lifestyle guidelines change with each season to continue supporting a life of presence and energetic engagement. The recommendations outlined below are specific to the spring season and will help balance *Kapha*.

Daily Routines for the Spring (*Kapha*) Season

Having taught *Ayurveda* since 2006, I often hear students discuss how they want to get rid of *Kapha* because it is associated with excess weight and Americans often have negative associations with fat. This understanding of *Kapha* is not complete. While it is true that *Kapha* is heavy, *Kapha* also creates the stability needed in this ever-changing world. This cleanse is designed to remove excess *Kapha* while fostering the beneficial qualities of *Kapha*.

Morning Routine

- Wake up around 6:00 am, but make sure to get at least 6 hours of sleep.
- Practice mindfulness, journal, or pray upon arising even if it is only for five minutes.
- Gently scrape your tongue as per the instructions provided later in this section.
- Drink 8-16 ounces (240-480 ml) of warm water. I like to put hot water in a thermos the night before, so it is warm when I wake up.

- Before you shower, perform *Garshana* (refer to Appendix III for additional information on how to do the silk glove massage). At the end of your morning shower, spend at least 20 seconds with cool or cold water running on your head and upper chest if possible.
- Exercise for at least 30-120 minutes (walking, yoga, etc.) to get the blood and the lymph fluid circulating.[4]

Mid-Day Routine

- Make lunch your primary meal of the day. This means your lunch is more substantial than your dinner. Ensure you feel satisfied with what and how much you have eaten.
- After lunch, consider resting (avoid lying down) or taking a 10-minute walk outside to aid digestion before returning to work.
- In the afternoon (2-4 hours after eating), do 5-20 minutes of exercise, or breathing practices.

Evening Routine

- 1 hour after dinner, or before bed, take 2 tablets of Triphala to help with morning elimination.
- Recapitulation: Write down or reflect on your day and how you interacted with people in your life.
- Turn off any flashing "rectangles" (T.V., phone, computer, etc.) after 7:30 pm.
- It will be most beneficial if you go to bed by 10:00 pm.

Please note that of the practices in the morning routine can be done at other times of the day. Try to finish all recommended daily activities before you go to sleep at night.

Monitor Your Tongue

The mouth is one of our first lines of defense when it comes to maintaining health and it is one of the places where *Kapha* accumulates. Poor oral hygiene can lead to imbalances. Monitoring your tongue is one way to keep track of your health, as it reflects the state of the digestive system and will provide information on how the cleanse is affecting your internal organs.

Tongue Monitoring

First, observe your tongue. Notice any variation in color, texture, coating, etc. That indicates how well you are digesting your food. Look for a slight coating on the tongue. If the coating is getting thicker, the foods you are choosing and the amounts you are eating are not supporting the Spring Ayurvedic Cleanse; change them to improve your results. Try to monitor your tongue at a similar time of day and commit the picture to memory so that you can compare it to next day. You may even want to take a picture of your tongue for comparison sake.

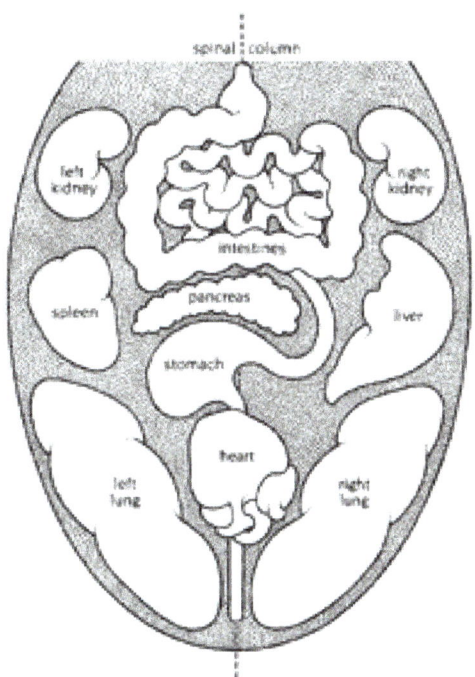

Tongue Scraping

As the tongue is connected to the digestive system a simple procedure can be used in order to gently stimulate digestion and help to remove ama from the body, this is called tongue scraping. Use a stainless-steel tongue cleaner and **gently** pull the uppermost coating off of the tongue. Remember to wash the scraper to remove the buildup. Repeat 3–5 times a session, or until very little buildup is present when washing the tongue cleaner.

Additional Preparation Recommendations

These additional recommendations will help you prepare for the cleanse by making the cleanse easier, thereby improving your level of success. For example, I go on a lot of backpacking trips and my enjoyment of the trip is directly proportionate to the amount of preparation I put in. If I don't prepare adequately, I often end up forgetting something essential, or the trip ends up being more stressful than it needs to be due to the absence of a plan. The Spring Cleanse works the same way. I suggest you read through these preparation recommendations, and include what will help you succeed.

- **Plan your meals ahead of time**

  - Anticipate that eating an elimination diet will take an extra 1-2 hours of food preparation time. Meals will take longer to prepare because you will be eliminating meat, dairy, soy, sugar, corn, caffeine, and wheat from your diet (as they are the most common food allergens, as well as inflammatory for the digestive process) and cooking more meals from scratch. I have included recipes for what to eat in the next part of the book. Look them over and decide if you want to use those recipes or use your own. Make a schedule of what you will be eating and make sure you have adequate time in your day to cook the food you need without feeling stressed. Alternatively, you could plan to cook some of your meals in advance.

- **Reduce your caffeine intake:** If you drink caffeine, cut back on caffeine incrementally in the weeks and days before you begin. For example, if you drink two or more cups of coffee every day, ease back to just one; then switch to half-caff; then decaf, yerba maté, or black tea. If you are a light coffee drinker, switch to green tea and then to herbal teas. The goal is to only drink herbal teas, green smoothies, and water during the two weeks of your Spring Ayurvedic Cleanse.

- **Tell your family and friends:** During the month, you will be eating specific meals and following specific practices. Let the people in your life know about your plans beforehand so they can support you. Who knows, you may even convince a person or two to join you.

- **Reduce your daily workload:** A major reason for doing the Spring Ayurvedic Cleanse is to reduce the amount of stress in your life. Before the starting day, look at your schedule and see where you can make some space. Cut out all non-essential commitments, even though it may mean saying "no" to some activities. Remember, you are only shifting things for a couple weeks.

- **Stock your kitchen and get cooking:** Make sure you have everything you need to prepare your food. This could be pantry items or appliances. Use the meal plans provided in this book or make your own. You might even try familiarizing yourself with some of the recipes before the cleanse starts so you are ready when the time comes.

- **Adjust your sleep schedule:** During the two weeks of your Spring Ayurvedic Cleanse, try to get to bed by 10:00 pm and wake up between 5:30 am–6:00 am. This sleep schedule supports optimal liver function, provides ample rest, and will give you enough time to do some yoga and meditation before you start the day.

- **Start growing Broccoli sprouts**. Follow the guidance in Appendix IV and get started making broccoli sprouts. Springtime is when our ancestors would traditionally eat a lot of sprouts and microgreens because young plants were available.

- **Start making Kraut.** Fermented vegetables are easy to make, and they are part of this program. Read Appendix V for instructions.

Digestive Tea to Improve Hydration

Get a 40-ounce, wide mouth stainless-steel thermos and fill with

- Boiled water,
- 1 Tablespoon of dried tulsi leaves or powder, and
- 1 Tablespoon of fennel seeds

Let cool until it is warm but drinkable. Sip 3-4 mouthfuls every 30 minutes throughout the day and aspire to drink 60 or more ounces of this tea a day. When you refill the thermos, you can leave the seeds inside and reuse them, using fresh seeds the following day. Make sure you are drinking 8 to 12 glasses (8 ounces each) of water a day through this and other methods. One strategy is to drink 8 ounces of water for every two hours you are awake, starting with at least two 8-ounce glasses of warm water in the morning before any food intake. Please note that hunger is often a sign of dehydration; if you feel hungry during this cleanse and are eating according to the schedule, you are likely dehydrated.

The Benefits of Drinking Water[57]

- Water dilutes and eliminates toxic accumulations.
- Water detoxifies our skin, kidneys, and improves our ability to sweat during exercise.
- Drinking water replaces the 48 to 64 ounces of water a day through urination, sweating, and breathing.
- Fatigue and headaches can be remedied by adequate water consumption.
- When we are hydrated our metabolism speeds up and is more efficient.
- Hydration decreases muscle and joint pain.

- Our brain operates better with water—our memory, concentration, and focus are all affected by water intake.

- Drinking water improves absorption of vital nutrients.

- Water transports nutrients to cells and tissues and transports wastes to the kidneys for filtration and elimination.

- Water retains and transports heat.

Summary of the Spring Ayurvedic Cleanse

All right! You've made it through Parts 1 and 2. In review, in Part 1 I covered why this program was developed and the goals. I introduced you to the fundamentals of *Ayurveda* that will be used during the cleanse. In Part 2 I outlined the dietary, herbal, and lifestyle guidelines you will need for the duration of the cleanse. Don't worry, you don't have to remember everything that has been covered up to this point; I will review it as we go.

The rest of the book will guide you step by step through the cleanse, and you can refer back to Parts 1 and 2 for any of the dietary, herbal, or lifestyle guidelines if needed. Ready? Let's begin!

Part 3: The Cleanse

DAY 1–3
Preparation Phase | GOAL: Remove

pg 95

pg 96

pg 97

pg 93

GUIDELINES FOR THE SPRING AYURVEDIC CLEANSE

Ayurvedic cleansing is often referred to as *Pancha karma*. The practices of *Pancha karma* were traditionally done over 30 days as an in-patient procedure. *Pancha karma* always consists of three phases: *poorva karma, pradhana karma,* and *paschat karma.* These are translated as preparation, main procedure, and integration. Many *Pancha karma* practices are now being offered in the West in an out-patient setting. While this has made them more accessible to the masses, it has also compromised their effectiveness.

This program is not *Pancha karma* and doesn't bear any resemblance to in-patient *Pancha karma* practices. The only similar element is how this program is broken down into three phases (although the second phase is broken down into two steps). Below is a basic preview of the upcoming three phases and what they will entail.

Guidelines for the Preparation Phase

As discussed before, the *Kapha Dosha* governs the stomach, pancreas, liver, and brain. Its qualities are heavy, cold, and damp. That is why stagnation is often used to describe a *Kapha* imbalance.

The preparation phase is focused on removing excess *Kapha*, specifically from the lungs and stomach. I have learned the best approach is from north to south: the lungs and stomach are above the pancreas and liver and so that is where we begin. Once the stomach and lungs are functioning better than we will be ready to move to the next phase.

Have you ever noticed when you eat too much you get congested? The congestion may even be bad enough that you are clearing the mucus from the back of your throat; mucus is associated with *Kapha*. In this phase we are removing the *Kapha* that created sluggish digestion in the stomach, causing mucus congestion in the mouth and sinus cavities. In addition to the dietary recommendations, herbal guidelines, and lifestyle guidelines covered earlier, there are specific recommendations that target the stomach to remove *Kapha*. These recommendations help to enkindle the production of enzymes that eliminate *Kapha* and improve the digestive fire.[58] As the coating on your tongue starts to diminish you will know you are removing excess *Kapha* in this phase.

Next are the specific recommendations for this phase in each of the five levels:

Physical

This phase stimulates the production of hydrochloric acid and improves digestion by removing *Ama* and excess *Kapha* from the body. This is done through the drinking of the lemon berry couli and the use of the *Kapha* churna on your food.[59,60] As you ignite the *Agni* in the stomach it starts to remove the *Kapha Ama* responsible for sluggish digestion, excess mucous, and excess weight. As *Ama* is removed, our stomach can break down the fats and proteins we eat so they can be better absorbed in the small intestine.

Mental/Emotional

Excess *Kapha* can create depression, lethargy, greed, possessiveness, or complacency. When these emotions and thoughts become habitual it is called emotional *Ama*. In this phase we work on removing the emotional *Ama* causing these thoughts and feelings. First, we must bring these feelings and thoughts to the surface by writing them down. You can do this process in one day or you can do it over the three days. Write down the emotions you consider emotional *Ama*. If you are not aware of the negative thoughts and emotions that rule your life, then I recommend monitoring your thoughts to notice what habitual ways of thinking are ruling your mind. Are you constantly complaining? Are you despondent? Do not judge these thoughts, just write them down. The goal is to get a list of the thoughts and emotions that you want to get rid of. Once you have your list, then either bury the list or place it in a river where it will be carried away. This symbolic gesture of letting go of these emotions and the ways in which they hold you back will help your body to understand that a change has, and will continue to, take place. As you let go of the list, imagine the thoughts and emotions being removed from your body and mind.

Spiritual

What is your relationship to your spiritual life? Do you meditate? Do you believe in a higher power? How do you connect with your deeper guidance and intuition? What gets in the way of connecting with your deeper essence? Take a moment now to answer these questions for yourself. An excess of *Kapha* can create a feeling of complacency. Or a feeling of being stuck. This feeling is usually associated with daily habits that take you away from your deeper self. For example, one barrier clients often identify is that busyness at work makes them feel so tired they don't wake up early enough to meditate in the morning. In this example, busyness is the barrier and meditation is what they would like to do more of. The next step is to develop a strategy to remove the barrier. Go to bed earlier, meditate later in the day, or taking on fewer projects at work are all possible responses. Whatever barriers you identify for yourself in this cleanse, know you only have to remove one barrier. In fact, resist the urge to try and remove too many barriers as this may become too much to do and, therefore, easy to not do at all. Instead, choose one and remove it, trusting that more barriers can be released at a later time.

Community

Community is one of the aspects of a whole person. Many of us currently feel lonely, even though we are surrounded by people and are connected through social media. *Kapha* can make you feel stuck in your patterns; in this phase, focus on identifying what, specifically, keeps you separate from the people and communities you love. Clients have offered the insights that they are too busy or don't feel motivated to leave the house. Trust your intuition, usually the first is correct. Whatever you identify as what keeps you separate is the barrier. Ask yourself what you long for in connection; the answer to this is your goal. Develop a plan to remove the barrier to reach your goal. Perhaps it is simple as enrolling in a class. Or maybe it is doing some research in a topic you enjoy. Prioritize connecting with local communities that are in-person instead of online communities, but any community will do.

Environmental

Many of us think of ourselves as separate from or superior to the Earth. When our relationships with the Earth are sick then we become sick. By removing the beliefs that we are separate from or superior to the Earth, we can start to reconnect with the Earth—and heal ourselves. *Kapha* is made of earth and water. It is our relationship with the ground beneath our feet and the water in our bodies that creates harmony. In order to re-establish harmony, we must restore our relationships with the soil and waterways. One way to do this is to see what items or practices in your home are harming the planet. It could be your consumption of plastic and non-reusable containers. It could be chemical laundry detergents or chemical-based fertilizers for your garden. Take stock of what you might be able to remove to help heal the planet, and then follow through. Remember, just choose one action, perhaps transitioning to all glass storage containers instead of plastic Tupperware, switching to biodegradable laundry soaps, or choosing products for your garden that uses organic materials.

Preparation Phase—Recommendations

1. **Physical** - Drink 1-4 glasses of lemon berry cooli and *Kapha* Churna.
2. **Emotional/mental** - Write down negative emotions or unhelpful thoughts you would like to get rid of and bury them or throw them in a river.
3. **Spiritual** - Identify, make a plan, and remove barriers that keep you from cultivating a more spiritual practices, like meditating and/or spending more time outside.
4. **Community** - Identify, make a plan, and remove any obstacles keeping you from either showing up more completely in existing communities or from joining new ones by dedicating at least one hour a week to a communal activity.
5. **Environmental** - Identify food you buy that is packaged in plastic and make a plan to find alternatives to this in order to remove the amount of plastic packaging you buy.

Preparation Phase Meal Suggestions

Breakfast

- ☐ Warm Zingy Green Smoothie
- ☐ Spring breakfast porridge

Lunch

- ☐ Tabbouleh salad
- ☐ Millet burgers

Dinner

- ☐ Beet borsht
- ☐ Green soup

Sample Meal Plan for the Preparation Phase

Day	Breakfast	Snack	Lunch	Snack	Dinner
Day 1	Warm Zingy Green Smoothie	Lemon Berry Cooli	Detox Tabbouleh salad	Lemon Berry Cooli	Beet Borsht
Day 2	Spring Breakfast Porridge	Lemon Berry Cooli	Millet burgers	Lemon Berry Cooli	Green Soup
Day 3	Warm Zingy Green Smoothie	Lemon Berry Cooli	Detox Tabbouleh salad	Lemon Berry Cooli	Beet Borsht

Preparation Phase—Specific Recipes

These recipes are intended as a guide and do not need to be followed to the letter. I created them based on what ingredients are best for reducing *Kapha*, however it is fine to substitute listed ingredients with what you have on hand. Feel free to omit or add things to the recipes so they fit your unique needs. Most important in this phase is to follow the general guidelines of eating lighter food that is not sweet, sour, or salty in order to balance *Kapha*.

For the purpose of clarity and to avoid any confusion for international readers, I have put down a list of basic cooking measurements:

> *1 US cup = 8 fluid ounces = 16 Tablespoons = 237 milliliters*
>
> *1 Tablespoon = 3 teaspoons = 1/2 ounce = 15 milliliters*
>
> *1 teaspoon = 1/6 ounce = 5 milliliters*

A NOTE about the recipes: All through high school and college, I made money by cooking in high-end restaurants. That means two things. One is that I never measure anything because measuring takes up valuable "food order" time. The other is that each recipe makes a lot of food. If you are a family of four, then the quantities might not be enough. But for less than four people, you will most likely have more than you need. That is why it is nice to cook with a friend or invite people over for dinner when you are making these recipes.

DAY 1–3 | SPECIFIC RECIPES

Lemon Berry Cooli
1 serving

- 1 whole lemon, juiced
- 12 ounces of water
- 1 handful berries – strawberries and raspberries
- 1 pinch of cayenne

Juice the lemon and remove the seeds. Place lemon juice in a blender, add water, cayenne, and berries. Blend and drink.

NOTE: You can drink up to 16 ounces (480 ml) of this elixir a day. For convenience, you can make a large batch to store in a half-gallon jar.

LEMON

The origin of the lemon is unknown, it's likely that they were first cultivated in north-western India over 2,500 years ago. The lemon showed up in Europe as ornamental plants in the 11th century and started being used as a culinary ingredient in the 15th century. Lemon's health benefits are due to vitamin C, B-vitamins (niacin, folate, thiamin, riboflavin), potassium, zinc, magnesium, and organic acids.

It was mentioned earlier that the goal of this phase is to increase the secretion of vital enzymes in the stomach as a first line of defense against pathogens and to ensure that every subsequent step in digestion is maximized. Lemons and lemon juice is one of the ways we accomplish this. Some of the benefits of lemons are:

- Fights bacteria and other pathogens. [61]
- Improved function of acid secreting parietal cells. [62]
- Better gastric emptying and reduced feeling of heaviness. [63]
- Improved liver function and detoxification.
- Improved weight loss.

Spring Churna

12 servings

Churna is a mixture of spices, herbs, and sometimes salts used in *Ayurvedic* cooking. Spices have long been used in *Ayurveda* to improve digestion. This *churna* is specific to the sluggish digestion found with *Kapha* imbalances.[78,79] It is also a great spice blend for most of the food presented in this recipe book.

- 1 Tablespoon fenugreek seeds
- 2 Tablespoons whole coriander seeds
- 1 Tablespoon whole mustard seed
- 1 Tablespoon ground ginger
- 1 Tablespoon ground turmeric
- 1 Tablespoon ground cinnamon
- 1 teaspoon ground clove

NOTE: You can also make this mix using powders if you don't want to blend the seeds in a spice grinder.

1. Blend the fenugreek, mustard, and coriander seeds in a spice grinder.
2. Mix all the ingredients in a bowl.
3. Store the spice blend in an airtight container, such as a glass jar.
4. Use 1-2 teaspoons while sautéing or cooking your meal. The flavor comes out best when you sprinkle the spice blend on ghee/oil as it heats up at the beginning of the recipe. Adding the *churna* early makes the spices more fragrant and removes their bitter taste.

DAY 1-3 | BREAKFAST RECIPES

Warm Zingy Green Smoothie
1-2 Servings

NOTE: This smoothie is thick, and you may need to chew it. If you can't tolerate the texture, consider using celery juice instead of the stalk, or omit celery all together.

- 2 handfuls destemmed kale or other leafy green vegetable
- Small piece of peeled ginger root
- 1 celery stick
- 4 ounces hot/warm water
- 4 ounces of warm apple juice
- Juice of 1 lemon

1. Hold the kale stem and pull the leaves from the stem.
2. Using the tip of a spoon's bowl, scrape the peel from a small piece of ginger, then slice the ginger into pieces.
3. Warm the water and apple juice in a pan on the stove.
4. Juice the lemon, removing any seeds.
5. Blend the kale, ginger, celery, apple, lemon, and water together. This smoothie is rather dense and may require consistent stirring.

DAY 1-3 | BREAKFAST RECIPES

Savory Millet Breakfast Porridge
1-2 Servings

- 1 Tablespoon sesame oil
- 1 teaspoon mustard seeds
- ¼ teaspoon garlic powder
- 1 teaspoon of winter spice *churna*

- ½ cup dry millet
- 1 cup of water
- 1 celery stalk, diced
- ¼ cup red cabbage, diced
- Salt to taste

Tip: You may want to ferment the millet by submerging it 8-16 hours in water with a splash of liquid from a jar of kraut or other fermented vegetables. Read more about this in Appendix II.

1. Place the sesame oil in a soup pot over medium high heat and add the winter spice *churna*, mustard, and garlic powder.
2. Add the millet, water, cabbage, and celery and cook on low heat for about 20 minutes.
3. Check consistency and add water if you like.

DAY 1-3 | LUNCH AND DINNER RECIPES

Millet Burgers
4-6 Burgers

Note: Burger substitutes tend to be time consuming and challenging. No matter how precisely you follow the recipe your burgers may not cook all the way through, or they may be too sticky or crumble too easily. If you are concerned about this, you may want to eat this meal as a porridge instead—it's also tasty!

- 1 cup cooked millet
- 1 ½ cups cooked black beans or 1 can black beans
- 2 Flax "eggs" (¾ cup hot water mixed with ¼ cup ground flax seeds, let sit 10 minutes)
- 1 Tablespoon winter spice *churna*
- 1 teaspoon cumin seeds
- 1 teaspoon pink Himalayan salt
- ¼ cup tapioca flour

1. Cook one cup of millet in two cups of water until all water is absorbed.
2. Cook 1 ½ cups of black beans in 4 cups of water in a pressure cooker, or use a can of black beans.
3. Preheat the oven to 350 degrees.
4. Mix the flax seed meal and hot water in a small bowl and set aside for 10 minutes.
5. In a medium-size bowl, add all ingredients.
6. Form into patties and place them on a sheet pan. Cook for 20 minutes at 350 degrees.

DAY 1-3 | LUNCH AND DINNER RECIPES

Detox Tabbouleh
4 servings

- 1 cup cooked quinoa
- 2 cups water
- 1 bunch parsley, minced
- 1 handful cilantro, minced
- 1 green onions, finely sliced
- 1 lemon, juiced
- 3 cloves garlic, minced
- 2 Tablespoons extra virgin olive oil
- ¼ teaspoon Himalayan salt

1. Cook 1 cup of quinoa in 2 cups of water. Once water is absorbed, remove from heat and let cool.
2. Finely chop the parsley and cilantro. Mince garlic, slice green onions.
3. In a medium-sized bowl, combine cooled quinoa, parsley, cilantro, garlic, onion, olive oil, and green onions.
4. Add salt to taste.

I used to make Tabouleh regularly and thought it was pretty good; everything changed when I dated a Lebanese woman. I remember the first time we made tabouleh and I learned to add generous amounts of parsley! We chopped parsley for at least 15 minutes. Despite being white quinoa, this recipe is green. Serve alone, or with soups, salads, or gluten free crackers. It is also great spooned over heartier dishes.

DAY 1-3 | LUNCH AND DINNER RECIPES

Green Soup
4 servings

- 1 Tablespoon sesame oil
- 2 medium-sized stalks of celery, chopped
- 1 medium-sized zucchinis, chopped
- 1 medium-sized bunch of a green leafy vegetable (e.g., spinach, chard, kale, arugula, etc.)
- 2 cups vegetable stock
- 1 Tablespoon coriander powder
- ⅛ teaspoon dry ginger powder
- Sea salt to taste

1. Blend all ingredients in a high-power blender.
2. Put all ingredients to a large soup pot and bring to a boil. Simmer for 5 minutes.
3. Finally, add salt to taste and serve.

Soured (Lacto-Fermented) Beets

- 6 small to medium beets
- Himalayan salt

1. Scrub the beets well, then cut off their tops and tails.
2. Grate the beets into a large bowl.
3. Add 3 Tablespoons (34 mL) salt per five pounds (2.2 kg) of grated beets. Mix well.
4. Stuff inside a crock or mason jar and let sit in a cupboard between one and four weeks (set an alarm on your phone so you don't forget), allowing the beets to ferment. Make sure the brine (liquid) is above the grated beets in order to avoid spoilage.
5. Once ready, the beets can be incorporated into the recipe below, omitting the red wine vinegar.

DAY 1-3 | LUNCH AND DINNER RECIPES

Beet Borsht
4-6 Servings

- 2-3 Tablespoons cultured ghee
- 1 large yellow onion, finely chopped
- 3-4 cloves garlic, minced
- 2 stalks celery, finely chopped
- 1 teaspoon caraway seeds
- 2 bay leaves
- 2 cups soured beets (recipe above) OR grated fresh beets
- 1 small red cabbage, grated
- 2 Tablespoon red wine vinegar (if not using soured beets)
- 4-5 cups vegetable stock

Borscht is traditionally made with soured, or lacto-fermented, beets.

1. In a large pot sauté the onion, garlic, and celery in ghee for about 7 minutes, stirring frequently. Add in the caraway and bay leaves and mix in.
2. Add soured or fresh beets and cabbage, and continue to sauté for 10-15 minutes, until the vegetables are soft.
3. If not using soured beets, add in the red wine vinegar and cook for another 5 minutes, and then add in the soup stock.
4. Bring to a boil, reduce to a simmer, and cook for 20 minutes if using soured beets and 45 minutes if using fresh beets.

Shopping List for the Preparation Phase (includes items from Pantry list, does not include final phase Kraut items)

GRAINS

- ❏ Organic millet
- ❏ Organic quinoa
- ❏ Tapioca flour

BEANS

- ❏ 1 can black beans or dried beans

NUTS AND SEEDS

- ❏ Flax seeds

OILS

- ❏ Organic unrefined sesame oil
- ❏ Organic extra virgin olive oil
- ❏ Organic avocado oil
- ❏ Organic cultured ghee

CONDIMENTS AND OTHER

- ❏ Red wine vinegar
- ❏ Stevia liquid
- ❏ Vegetable stock

FRUITS

- ❏ 6 lemons
- ❏ 1 pint berries
- ❏ 1 quart apple juice

DAY 1-3 | SHOPPING LIST

HERBS AND SPICES

- ☐ 6 inches of fresh ginger
- ☐ 2 cloves garlic
- ☐ Bay leaves
- ☐ Caraway seeds
- ☐ Cayenne pepper powder
- ☐ Chili powder
- ☐ Cinnamon powder
- ☐ Clove powder
- ☐ Coriander powder
- ☐ Coriander seeds
- ☐ Cumin powder
- ☐ Cumin seeds
- ☐ Curry powder
- ☐ Fenugreek seeds
- ☐ Garam Masala
- ☐ Granulated garlic powder
- ☐ Ginger powder
- ☐ Asafoetida (Hing)
- ☐ Mustard powder
- ☐ Mustard seeds
- ☐ Turmeric powder
- ☐ Salt

VEGETABLES

- ☐ 1 bunch kale
- ☐ 1 medium red cabbage
- ☐ 2 medium-sized red beets
- ☐ 1 head of celery
- ☐ 1 bunch of parsley
- ☐ 1 bunch cilantro
- ☐ 1 bunch scallions (green onion)
- ☐ 1 yellow onion
- ☐ 1 bunch spinach or other leafy greens
- ☐ 1 medium sized zucchini

DAY 4-7
Main Phase: Step One (4 days) | GOAL: Repair

Guidelines for the Main Cleanse: Step One

In the phase before you used the lemon berry cooli and spring *churna* to ignite digestion in the stomach. You also focused on removing obstacles in other areas of your life. As we move North to South within the digestive tract, our next *Kapha* organ is the pancreas. The pancreas' job is to breakdown fat and starch to turn it into the body's fuel in the form of glucose. The pancreas then secretes insulin in order to use the fuel. When there is too much *Kapha*, the body stores the created fuel as fat instead of utilizing it. In this phase the goal is to repair the pancreas and to remove the obstructions caused by *Kapha*. This leads to improved energy and stamina.

This is done by doing a traditional *Ayurvedic* cleanse, using a food called *Kichari* (pronounced kich-uh-ree). In other books and resources, you may see this food spelled as *Kitchari* or *Kichadi*. After the profound cleansing in a *Pancha karma* cleanse, the body's digestion can be unstable. *Kitchari* is used after one of the five strong cleansing actions in order to reboot and reset the digestion and provide needed nourishment without overwhelming the digestive fire. Although you are not doing one of the five strong cleansing actions you can use this food here to support digestion.

Next are the specific recommendations for this phase in each of the five levels.

Physical

Kitchari is a porridge-like dish that *Ayurveda* relies on to sustain the body during purification. *Kitchari* means "mixture," and usually consists of one grain and one bean. For most people, *Kitchari* is a nourishing and easy-to-digest meal that works great as a staple food. Although traditionally made with white basmati rice and yellow split mung beans, *Kitchari* can be made with any grain and bean combination. The recipes in this cleanse will be using the same grain and bean combo (quinoa and yellow split mung dahl) for all the recipes for convenience. Remember you can substitute any grain or bean that you prefer. When this grain and bean combination is mixed with ghee or another oil, spices, and leafy green vegetables, it provides the essential carbohydrates, protein, and fatty acids needed to sustain the body.

Kitchari eliminates any confusion or second-guessing that arises around what to eat, and helps you avoid the questionable foods in your diet known to produce *Ama*. *Kitchari* is *Ama*-reducing by providing essential nourishment.[75]

To optimize the function of the pancreas you will be making your own broccoli sprouts and including them with your *kitchari*. Hopefully, you have already started sprouting them and they are ready to go for this phase. If not, you can usually purchase the sprouts at the grocery store. For more information on how broccoli sprouts support the digestive organs, see Appendix IV.

In this phase you will also be drinking the apple cider vinegar elixir. Vinegar ignites the digestive fire in the stomach and pancreas and helps to clear *Kapha* from the body.[64] The pinch of cayenne gives the elixir a little kick so you can start to repair the pancreas function and optimize the body's ability to break down food.

> **NOTE:** Some people have a hard time digesting grains and beans due to the lectin content. If you suffer from that issue, ensure that you are pressure cooking your beans and fermenting your grains. If you don't know how to ferment grains, refer to Appendix II. If you continue to have problems with digestion, revert to the recipes in any of the other phases.

Emotional/Mental

Repair your *Kapha* emotions in this phase. Common *Kapha* emotions are greed, attachment, excess desire, depression, and lethargy. Integration of emotions bring healing. In my work with clients, I witness that many stuck emotions developed in childhood. Remember that *Kapha* rules this phase of life. There may have been specific events that led to the unhelpful emotions listed above.

Settle into a comfortable and safe place with your journal. Free-write for fifteen minutes and see if you can identify if any of your unhelpful *Kapha* emotions began in childhood, noting specifically when they arose; usually, these emotions were used to provide protection when you were feeling unsafe. Next, invite your current adult self to the scene. Write how your adult self extends love to the child that was hurt and who developed these *Kapha* emotions as a protective strategy. Sometimes this exercise works well as a dialogue form, other times as poetry or as drawings. You are taking the steps to be the protective adult you needed then.

The best way to thoroughly uncover and repair these emotions is through counseling. This cleanse is not meant to be a replacement for one-on-one therapy, but it is meant to bring more awareness to these emotions so that they can be repaired. During this cleanse you can start to uncover the places within yourself that have been wounded and start to re-parent them safely.

Spiritual

Over the winter, you may have gotten distracted by the *Kapha* emotions of greed and desire. When this happens, you lose track of the connection with your own inner compass. Alignment with your compass is the essence of your constitution. By recognizing your constitution, or *Prakruti* as introduced before, you are in alignment with your true nature and deepest calling.

In this second phase of the cleanse, choose one modality to use in order to work toward repairing your inner compass. This can look a lot of different ways. You could meditate more to better hear the voice of your inner guidance. You could spend more time in nature. You could make art, write, or dance. You could actively practice trusting your intuition more. Whatever you choose, ensure that it helps you to repair your relationship with your inner guidance system.

Community

Repair your relationship with a community you have been part of. Community can be family, friend groups, social groups, or others. Repair means finding what is not working with how you connect with that community and consciously making the changes so you can be in connection and get your needs met at the same time.

To identify the places that might need repair I'll review some of the aspects of *Kapha*. *Kapha* is responsible for protection and lubrication in the body. It protects our stomach, joints, and other parts of the body by keeping them moist and fluid. When there is too much *Kapha* you can feel stuck in place and unable to move forward. *Kapha* resides in the chest and so it can often lead to a closed down heart. This extra insulation *Kapha* creates around the heart can hinder your ability to connect with community. When there is too much *Kapha* you distance yourself from others. Are you protecting your heart and no longer able to be vulnerable with certain people in your community? How is this affecting the entire community? Close your eyes and listen to your intuition as you ask yourself, what is needed to repair this relationship and community? The goal here is to identify who is part of your current community and what type of repair is needed. Find a community you have pushed away and begin repairing your relationship.

Environmental

Kapha is ruled by the elements of water and earth and repairing your relationship with the planet will help to balance *Kapha*. We each live in different places. Some are more wet, and others are dry. Some of us live in places with a back yard and others live in apartments in cities. The way in which you repair your relationship to water and soil is unique to your situation. If you live somewhere dry, find ways to conserve water. If you live somewhere with space, plant a garden. If you already have a garden, take out invasive plants. If you live in an urban space, pick up trash. Choose something you can follow through on, and something that is in direct context with your local ecosystem and community.

Main Phase: Step One—Recommendations

1. **Physical** - Eat *Kitchari* with Quinoa for 3 meals each day with sprouts. Drink ACV elixir
2. **Emotional/mental** - Reparent the inner child parts of yourself that have been wounded by identifying one childhood memory and three things/feelings that are needed to heal the wound from that.
3. **Spiritual** - Repair your relationship with Spirit by finding a prayer, guided meditation, visualization, or poem that helps you connect to your deeper essence.
4. **Community** - Look at the communities you are a part of and identify if repair is needed. Is there discomfort, frustration, or confusion in any of your relationships? If so, repair this by identifying what you can do to bring more comfort, acceptance, and clarity to this community.
5. **Environmental** - Repair your relationship with water by investing in practices and infrastructure that conserve water.

Main Cleanse Phase: Step One—Meal Suggestions

Breakfast

- ❏ Apple cider vinegar elixir
- ❏ Simple *Kichari*
- ❏ Quinoa *Kichari*

Lunch and Dinner

- ❏ East Indian *Kichari*
- ❏ *Kapha* reducing *Kichari*
- ❏ Spicy *Kichari*
- ❏ Coconut and shitake *Kichari*
- ❏ Rosemary basil *Kichari*
- ❏ *Kichari* dumplings

Sample Meal Plan for the Main Phase: Step 1

Day	Breakfast	Snack	Lunch	Snack	Dinner
Day 4	Simple *Kichari*	ACV Elixir	*Kapha* reducing *Kichari*	ACV Elixir	Spicy *Kichari*
Day 5	Quinoa *Kichari*	ACV Elixir	Rosemary basil *Kichari*	ACV Elixir	Coconut and shitake *Kichari*
Day 6	Simple *Kichari*	ACV Elixir	*Kapha* reducing *Kichari*	ACV Elixir	East Indian *Kichari*
Day 7	Quinoa *Kichari*	ACV Elixir	Rosemary basil *Kichari*	ACV Elixir	*Kichari* dumplings

DAY 4–7 | SPECIFIC RECIPES

A LOOK AHEAD

You will need fermented vegetables (krauts) for the final phase of this program. I recommend making them ahead of time, using the recipes found in the Integration Phase section. The krauts take about 10 days to be ready and up to six weeks to be full of the most probiotics. It is a good skill to learn and it's easier than you think!

You may also want to start growing broccoli sprouts and starting your inoculum for fermenting your grains. Both covered in the Appendix II and IV to this book.

ACV (Apple Cider Vinegar) Elixir
1 Serving

- 1 Tablespoon apple cider vinegar (raw and unpasteurized)
- 5 drops liquid stevia (lemon-flavored is my favorite)
- 1¼ cups filtered water
- 1 pinch cayenne powder

NOTE: You can drink up to 16 ounces (480 ml) of this elixir a day. For convenience, you can make a large batch and store it in a half-gallon jar.

Mix all the ingredients and serve.

DAY 4-7 | SPECIFIC RECIPES

Broccoli Sprouts

BROCCOLI SPROUTS GROWING INSTRUCTIONS

1. Add two Tablespoons of broccoli seeds, such as Food to Live Organic Broccoli Seeds, to a wide-mouthed glass quart jar. Cover with a few inches of filtered water and cap with the sprouting lid. Store in a warm, dark place overnight.

2. The next morning (or at least eight hours later), drain off the water and rinse with fresh water.

3. Place the sprouting jar upside down at a 45-degree angle on a sprouting jar stand. Place in warm and dark place.

4. Rinse and drain the sprouts in the morning and evening (don't forget as rinsing the sprouts stops them from growing bacteria), placing them back in the jar holder after each rinse. After a few days the seeds will break open. After about five days the sprouts will be about an inch long. If the sprouts start to smell funny then they weren't rinsed frequently enough or they got too hot, throw them away and start over.

5. Next, place the seeds next to a window where they can get indirect sunlight. When the leaves become dark green they are ready to eat. The whole process takes a week.

6. Once the sprouts are ready to eat you will want to store them. Wait about 12 hours from the last rinse so all the remaining moisture has drained off, then replace the sprouting lids with a regular mason jar lid. Place them in the refrigerator and try to eat all of them in the first three to four days. If you do not eat them all, compost them; sprouts go badly quickly.

DAY 4-7 | SPECIFIC RECIPES

A Note About *Kichari*

Make a large amount of quinoa and split mung dal at one time (see recipe below). From those large quantities, divide the quinoa and split mung dal and use them in the individual recipes below. On average, one cup of dry quinoa will make three servings and one cup of uncooked mung dal will make two servings once cooked. If you decide not to pre-cook everything, you can find a lot of *Kichari* recipes online using uncooked beans and grains.

I use quinoa and split mung dal in my recipes because they are light, which balances the *Kapha Dosha*. If you decide to use a different grain/bean combo, ensure the ones you choose are also light in nature.

Lastly, *Kichari* is not meant to be the best tasting food on the planet. It is meant to give you the nourishment your body needs—not your tongue. *Kichari* will give you a chance to tune in to your natural appetite again. Instead of desiring food because it tastes good you will begin to want food because you are hungry, and specific foods because of the nutrients and minerals your body needs to function.

Cooking split mung dal

1. Soak the split mung dal for at least 8 hours prior to cooking.
2. Add 3 cups of soaked split mung dal and 7 cups of water into a pressure cooker. I use an InstaPot. Use the beans setting and set the time to 7. Once cooked, you may have to drain off excess water.
3. Place two Rapunzel bouillon cubes and 1 Tablespoon of sesame oil in with the beans and stir until incorporated.

Cooking quinoa

1. Soak 6 cups of quinoa in the inoculum for 8 hours (See Appendix II for more information on the inoculum and how to work with grains).
2. Strain the quinoa and reserve some inoculum.
3. Place the 6 cups of quinoa and 6 cups of water into a soup pot. Bring water to a boil, then reduce to a simmer. Cook for about 10 minutes until all the water is absorbed.

Note about spice blends: Most of the ingredients in these recipes are spices. It can be helpful to have your own spice blends. (Remember back to the last phase where you made the Spring Cleanse *Churna*? That is a wonderful spice mix to use if you prefer not to measure everything out each time.) Or you can buy curry powder, chili powder, and other spice blends and use those instead of the spices listed in the recipes.

DAY 4-7 | LUNCH AND DINNER RECIPES

Simple *Kichari*
1-2 Servings

- 1 Tablespoon sesame oil
- 1 teaspoon mustard seeds, brown, yellow, or black
- 1 teaspoon cumin seeds
- ¼ teaspoon cardamom powder
- ¼ teaspoon clove powder
- ¼ teaspoon turmeric
- 3 bay leaves
- ½ cup cooked quinoa
- ½ cup cooked split yellow mung dal
- ½ cup shredded carrot
- 1 handful dinosaur kale, sliced
- ¼ cup frozen peas
- 1 small handful cilantro
- ¼ teaspoon salt

DAY 4-7 | LUNCH AND DINNER RECIPES

1. Pour the sesame oil into a medium sized saucepan and turn the heat to medium high.
2. Add the mustard and cumin seeds. When they start to brown add the cardamom, clove, turmeric, and bay leaves. Stir in.
3. Add the cooked quinoa and mung dal.
4. Add ⅛ cup of water to help the spices mix with the quinoa and dal and to stop it from sticking to the pan. You may have to add more water as you go to prevent sticking.
5. After about 5 minutes the grains and beans should be warm. Add the carrot, kale, peas, and cilantro. Cook for another 5 minutes or until all ingredients are warm.
6. Add the salt and then serve with broccoli sprouts.

ADDITIONAL INFORMATION ON MUSTARD

Mustard belongs to the same family as broccoli and cabbage. It is native to Europe and it has been used around the world. There are many varieties of mustard with very similar properties. These are white mustard (*Brassica alba,*) black mustard (*Brassica nigra*), and brown mustard (*Brassica juncea*). White and yellow mustard is the traditional condiment and brown mustard is used in Dijon mustard. In this phase we will primarily be using the mustard seed. Some of its benefits are:

- Anti-inflammatory, especially for the skin.[66,67]
- Balances the blood sugar.
- Improve gall bladder function.

DAY 4-7 | LUNCH AND DINNER RECIPES

Quinoa *Kichari*
1-2 Servings

- 1 Tablespoon sesame oil
- 1 teaspoon mustard seeds, brown, yellow, or black
- 1 teaspoon cumin seed
- 2 or 3 Tablespoons fresh ginger, minced
- 1 Tablespoon curry powder or turmeric powder
- ¼ cup burdock root, sliced
- ¼ cup broccoli, chopped
- ½ cup cooked split yellow mung dal
- ½ cup cooked quinoa
- ½ cup chard, sliced
- ½ Tablespoon salt
- 1 cup cilantro

1. Pour the sesame oil into a medium sized saucepan and turn the heat to medium high.
2. Add the mustard seeds and cumin seeds. When they start to brown, add the fresh ginger and curry powder or turmeric. Stir.
3. Add the burdock root and broccoli. Cook another few minutes. You may need to add water so the spices don't burn.
4. Add the cooked quinoa and mung dal and cook about five minutes, stirring frequently until the mixture is warm. You may need to add another splash of water so the grains and beans don't stick in the pan.
5. Add the chard, salt, and cilantro. Cook for another five minutes.
6. Remove from heat and serve with broccoli sprouts.
7. Optional: Add a splash of lemon or coconut aminos.

Kapha-Reducing Kitchari

1–2 Servings

- 1 teaspoon ghee or sesame oil
- ½ teaspoon of black mustard seeds
- 1 teaspoon cumin seeds
- 1 teaspoon peeled, fresh grated ginger
- ½ teaspoon of turmeric
- 3 bay leaves
- 1 teaspoon curry powder
- ¼ cup leek, chopped
- ¼ cup golden beet, shredded
- 1 cup green beans, chopped
- ½ cup cooked quinoa
- ½ cup cooked split mung beans
- 1 cup dinosaur kale, sliced
- 1 teaspoon sea salt

1. Place the ghee or pour the sesame oil into a medium sized saucepan, then turn the heat to medium high.
2. Add the mustard seeds and cumin seeds. When the seeds brown or pop, add the fresh ginger, turmeric, ginger, bay leaves, and curry powder.
3. After a few minutes add the leeks, golden beet, and green beans. Cook for 5–10 minutes, stirring often. Add water if the spices start to burn.
4. Add the cooked quinoa and mung beans, and cook for five minutes or until warm. Add water if beans or grains start to stick to the pan.
5. Add the kale and salt, cook for another 5 minutes.
6. Optional: Add a splash of lemon or coconut aminos.
7. Remove from heat and serve with broccoli sprouts.

DAY 4-7 | LUNCH AND DINNER RECIPES

Rosemary and Basil Kitchari
1-2 Servings

- 1 Tablespoon avocado oil
- 1 teaspoon mustard seeds, brown, yellow, or black
- 1 teaspoon dried rosemary or 1 Tablespoon fresh
- ¼ teaspoon black peeper
- 3 bay leaves
- 2 cloves of garlic, minced
- ¼ cup leek, diced
- ½ cup celery, diced
- ½ cup cooked split yellow mung dal
- ½ cup cooked quinoa
- 1 Tablespoon dried basil or 3 Tablespoons fresh basil
- 1 teaspoon oregano
- 1 cup spinach, chopped
- ¼ teaspoon salt

1. Pour the avocado oil into a medium sized saucepan and turn the heat to medium high.
2. Add the mustard seeds, rosemary, black pepper, and bay leaves. Cook until the mustard seeds pop, about 3 minutes.
3. Then add the minced garlic, leek, and celery, and cook for five minutes. Add water if spices start to burn.
4. Add cooked quinoa and split mung dal, and cook until warm about 5 minutes. Add a splash of water if the quinoa or split mung dal begin to stick to the pan.
5. Add basil, oregano, spinach, and salt. Stir. When spinach is wilted then remove from heat. Serve with broccoli sprouts.

Spicy Kitchari

1-2 Servings

- 1 Tablespoons ghee or sesame oil
- 1 teaspoon mustard seeds, brown, yellow, or black
- 4 cloves garlic, minced
- 1 small jalapeno, deseeded and minced
- 1 Tablespoon chili powder
- 2 green onions, diced
- 1 small zucchini, diced
- ½ cup cooked split yellow mung dal
- ½ cup cooked quinoa
- 1 Tablespoon dried oregano
- 1 cup arugula, chopped
- ½ teaspoon salt
- Optional: cilantro, avocado, lime juice

1. Place the ghee or pour the sesame oil into a large saucepan on medium heat, then add the mustard seeds. When they pop, sauté the garlic and jalapeno for about 5 minutes, or until the garlic is golden brown.
2. Add chili powder and green onion and sauté for another 3 minutes.
3. Add the zucchini and cook for 5 minutes.
4. Add quinoa and mung and cook until warm, about 5 minutes. You'll most likely need to add a little water so the quinoa does not stick to the pan.
5. Add the oregano and arugula.
6. Add salt and remove from heat. Serve with broccoli sprouts.

DAY 4-7 | LUNCH AND DINNER RECIPES

Coconut and Shitake Kitchari
1-2 Servings

- 1-2 Tablespoons coconut oil
- 1 teaspoon mustard seeds, brown, yellow, or black
- 1 small piece ginger, diced small
- 4 cloves of garlic, minced
- ¼ cup leek, diced
- ¼ of green cabbage, sliced
- 1 handful shitake mushrooms, sliced
- ½ cup cooked split yellow mung dal
- ½ cup cooked quinoa
- 1 Tablespoon Thai red curry paste
- 1 baby bok choy
- Juice of 1 lime
- ½ teaspoon salt

1. Place the coconut oil in a large saucepan on medium heat, then add mustard seeds. When they pop, sauté the ginger and garlic for about 5 minutes, or until the garlic is golden brown.
2. Add the leek, shitake mushrooms, and cabbage.
3. Sauté for five minutes.
4. Add the cooked mung dal and quinoa. Then add some water and the red curry paste. Cook for a few more minutes until the mixture is warm.
5. Add the bok choy and juice of the lime.
6. Remove from heat, add salt, and serve with broccoli sprouts.

DAY 4-7 | LUNCH AND DINNER RECIPES

East Indian Kitchari
1-2 Servings

- 1-2 Tablespoons ghee or sesame oil
- 1 teaspoon black mustard seeds
- 1 teaspoon cumin seeds
- 1 Tablespoon fresh minced ginger
- 1 Tablespoon curry powder
- ¼ teaspoon fenugreek
- ½ cup yellow onion, diced
- ¼ cup celery, diced
- ½ cup cooked split yellow mung dal
- ½ cup cooked quinoa
- ¼ cup zucchini, diced
- ½ cup broccoli, diced
- ½ teaspoon salt

1. Place the ghee or pour the sesame oil into a large saucepan on medium heat. Add mustard seeds and cumin seeds, then cook until the seeds pop or become fragrant.
2. Add the ginger, curry powder, and fenugreek and cook for a few minutes until fragrant.
3. Add the diced onion and saute for a few more minutes until they become more translucent clear. Add water if needed.
4. Add the celery, dal, and quinoa, then stir until the mixture is warm, adding water so it doesn't stick.
5. Add the zucchini and broccoli. Cook for a few more minutes.
6. Remove from heat, add salt and serve. Serve with broccoli sprouts.

DAY 4-7 | LUNCH AND DINNER RECIPES

Kitchari Dumplings
1-2 Servings

I can get bored of eating *Kichari* as a porridge; this recipe is meant to inspire you to play around with the consistency of the *Kichari*. You can do this with any of the previous recipes, just make sure the veggies are well chopped so the dumplings stay together better.

- 2 Flax "eggs" (¾ cup hot/warm water mixed with ¼ cup ground flax seeds, let sit 10 minutes)
- 1 cup *Kitchari*
- ¼ cup chickpea, rice, or coconut flour
- Additional salt or spices

1. Preheat the oven to 375.
2. Stir the flaxseed into the warm water. Let sit for 10 minutes, then add to the *Kitchari*.
3. Add the flour slowly until the texture forms easily into small balls.
4. Shape the balls into patties if you wish, then place them on a sheet pan. You can use a spoon or your hands for this.
5. Place the tray in the oven and cook for 15-20 minutes until golden brown on the outside. (Remember, they are already cooked!)
6. Remove and eat as balls or patties, or you can place them in a romaine lettuce leaf and eat them like a falafel.
7. Serve with broccoli sprouts.

Shopping List for the Main Cleanse Phase:
Step One (includes items from Pantry list)

GRAINS AND SEEDS

- ☐ 3-5 cups white quinoa
- ☐ 1 cup ground flax seeds
- ☐ 1 cup chickpea, rice, or coconut flour

BEANS

- ☐ 3-5 cups split yellow mung beans

OILS AND VINEGAR

- ☐ Organic unpasteurized apple cider vinegar
- ☐ Organic extra virgin coconut oil
- ☐ Organic avocado oil
- ☐ Organic grass-fed cultured ghee
- ☐ Organic unrefined sesame oil

CONDIMENTS AND OTHER

- ☐ Thai red curry paste
- ☐ Vegetable bouillon cubes
- ☐ Liquid stevia, preferably with lemon

FRUITS

- ☐ 1-2 limes

DAY 4-7 | SHOPPING LIST

HERBS AND SPICES

- ☐ 6 inches of fresh ginger
- ☐ 2 garlic bulbs
- ☐ Mustard seeds, black, yellow, or brown
- ☐ Cayenne pepper powder
- ☐ Cumin seed
- ☐ Cardamom powder
- ☐ Clove powder
- ☐ Turmeric powder
- ☐ Bay leaves
- ☐ Fennel seeds
- ☐ Coriander seeds
- ☐ Basil, dried leaves
- ☐ Oregano, dried leaves
- ☐ Rosemary, dried leaves
- ☐ Chili powder
- ☐ Curry powder
- ☐ Fenugreek powder
- ☐ Black pepper
- ☐ Salt

VEGETABLES

- ☐ Broccoli sprout seeds
- ☐ 2 bunches dinosaur kale
- ☐ 1 bunch cilantro
- ☐ 1 4-inch piece burdock root
- ☐ 1 broccoli head
- ☐ 1 head of celery
- ☐ 1 bunch chard
- ☐ 1 medium sized leek
- ☐ 1 golden beet
- ☐ 1 bunch green onion
- ☐ 1 handful green beans
- ☐ 1 bunch spinach
- ☐ 1 bunch arugula
- ☐ 1 small jalapeno
- ☐ 2 zucchinis
- ☐ 1 bunch arugula
- ☐ 1 baby bok choy
- ☐ 1 cup shitake mushrooms
- ☐ 1 small carrot
- ☐ ½ head green cabbage
- ☐ 1 medium yellow onion
- ☐ 1 bag frozen peas

DAY 8–10
Main Phase: Step Two (3 days) | GOAL: Restore

pg 138
pg 133
pg 136
pg 135

Guidelines for the Main Cleanse, Phase Two

In the last phase you were using *Kichari*, broccoli sprouts, and the apple cider vinegar elixir to improve pancreatic function and repair the digestive tract. In this phase you will restore the healthy functioning of *Kapha* in the digestive tract beginning with the liver. *Kapha*'s job in the liver is to synthesize cholesterol, proteins, bile, and hormones. In this phase we will be giving the liver a much-needed break, which will allow it to restore its normal functions. I think of the liver like a janitor who comes into your body after hours to clean up. If you have been overeating for decades, the janitor can never fully catch up. By using calorie restriction, you can finally restore liver function and allow the janitor to catch up.

Next are the specific recommendations for this phase in each of the five levels.

Physical: Calorie Restriction

Kapha imbalances respond well to fasting. While I am a big proponent of fasting, I am recommending calorie restriction here instead since this is a book and cannot include the personal guidance and oversight needed when fasting. Long stretches of fasting can lead to medical challenges if not executed well. Calorie restriction, however, has been used by traditional cultures around the world for thousands of years.

Term	Definition
Fasting	Complete avoidance of calorie intake from anywhere between one day to several weeks
Calorie Restriction	20–40% reduction in caloric intake over a long period of time (1200 calories for women vs. 1400 calories for men per day)
Intermittent Fasting	Complete avoidance of calorie intake for 16–18 hours daily, or alternating a fasting day (usually a 24-hour fast) with a normal calorie intake day

In this phase you will reduce daily caloric intake by 30%. The number of calories you reduce depends on the number of calories you usually expend in a day by reducing the amount you eat by 30%. If you are used to eating an average of 2,000 calories per day, you reduce that to 1,400 calories per day.

There are a few ways to do this. One is outright calorie restriction, meaning you eat less at every meal. The second way is a time-restricted feeding routine, also known as intermittent fasting. When intermittently fasting, an individual only eats during eight of the 24 hours in a day, such as between 11 am and 8 pm. Most people gradually move into this, starting with a 10/14 schedule, where they don't eat for 10 hours and eat only within a 14-hour window (e.g. only eating between 6am and 8pm). From there, they progress to 12/12 (e.g., only eating between 8 am and 8 pm), then to 14/10 (e.g., only eating between 8 am and 6 pm), and to 16/8 (e.g., only eat between 11 am and 7 pm) and lastly to a 18/6 (e.g., only eat between 12 am and 6 pm). You get the most benefits when you are avoiding calorie intake for 16–18 hours over a few days. The goal is to reduce calories. How you do that in this cleanse is up to you.

In the modern world, people commonly eat too much. Your digestive system is working overtime, and constantly breaking down, digesting, absorbing, and assimilating food in a never-ending fashion. In the rest of the animal kingdom, this does not happen. Animals instinctively know that taking breaks from eating is important, as it allows the body's energy to be diverted to cleaning house—clearing toxins and repairing cells, etc. in a process known as autophagy—instead of digesting. Digestion takes a lot of energy, which could alternatively be used for many important clean-up functions in the body.

To assist with your calorie restriction goals, use a calorie counting app if you would like. They can be confusing though, so try a few out to find one that works for you.

> I have found the Meal Snap (iOS) and MyNetDiary apps are decent for counting calories.

I have personally stopped using calorie counting apps due to the potentially obsessive atmosphere they create. The approach I use now is a nutrition-intuition approach. I don't know how many calories I consume in a day, but I do know how much I generally eat in terms of bowls of food. Since I prefer to use the time-restricted feeding option, I skip dinner. And for my other meals, I fill a slightly smaller bowl of food as compared to the bowl I normally use. This seems to do the trick for me. I hope you can come up with a similar method that works for you and helps you reduce how much you normally eat by 30%. By reducing calories, you allow your body to flush out the *Ama* that remains in your system.[68,69] This process may not remove all the *Ama* present in your body, but it will clean out toxins that generally weaken your *Agni*, or digestive forces.

Emotional/Mental

During this phase of the Spring Cleanse, you will have the opportunity to restore positive *Kapha* emotions. To repeat, examples of less-desirable *Kapha* emotions are lazy, depressed, stuck, unmotivated, attached, and greedy. In the last couple phases, you have been using practices to help remove and repair these emotions. In this step you will restore the positive emotions associated with *Kapha*, such as gratitude, compassion, patience, and love.

In this cleanse, I will specifically guide you towards focusing on the emotion of gratitude. Be aware of the things that you are grateful for. One way to do this is to have a gratitude journal. Write down three things that you are grateful for every day. Many of us use food to soothe uncomfortable emotions. Focusing on what you are grateful for during this phase can provide the soothing that you may have used food for in the past.

Spiritual

This is an opportunity to restore your commitment to your spirit. If you are interested in *Ayurveda*, it is likely you have a spiritual life or are involved in spiritual practices. When *Kapha* is in excess those practices can become routine or rote. You may find you are doing the practices but they do not have the same effect they once did, and you may not be feeling enlivened and awakened by those practices anymore. *Kapha* requires stimulation and new energy to break through old patterns. In order to restore your commitment to spirit, try new things and stimulate yourself in new ways. This could be a breathing practice, a chant, a visualization. Let your intuition guide you to what feels right to try. If you are new to spiritual practices, start by meditating, praying, or spending time in nature for at least twenty minutes a day.

Community

At this time, be intentional about restoring your commitment to community gatherings. With too much *Kapha*, you can become sluggish and stop attending spaces of community. Or perhaps you are already committed to an in-person community gathering, but you have been arriving late, leaving early, or being distracted on your phone—in other words, you haven't been fully showing up. If that's the case, then recommit to being fully present.

In order to restore the beneficial aspects of community in your life, it is important to invest time and energy in the people around you. If *Kapha* is in excess, it can be challenging to shift the energy and get off the couch. In this case, gift yourself a more active community gathering as your first re-entry, such as a group exercise class or a rowdy board game night with good friends. Sometimes all that is needed to shift the *Kapha* energy is enough stimulation to start doing something new. Once you have committed, then gathering with people usually becomes easy to sustain over time.

Environmental

Restoring your relationship with the land is a paramount part of this cleanse, as *Ayurveda* is rooted in nature. Do you have a relationship to the land you live on? If not, then it is time to connect to the land beneath your feet. This could be as simple as finding a place at which you sit daily and admire the land, noting the change of seasons. Or perhaps you feel motivated to revive your garden by planting flowers or vegetables. It is the springtime, so this is a great time to be in the garden. Remember that, no matter what you do for this Restore phase, notice the small details through your senses. Find ways to restore your relationship with the place you live.

Main Phase, Step Two— Specific Recommendation

1. **Physical** - Follow a calorie restricted diet.
2. **Emotional/Mental** - Each day, write down three things for which you are grateful.
3. **Spiritual** - Restore your commitment to a vibrant spiritual life by meditating, praying, or spending time in nature for at least twenty minutes a day.
4. **Community** - Restore your reserves by attending a community gathering every week.
5. **Environmental** - Connect with the land on which you live: tend the soil, plant a garden, or do something that helps you get to know the land intimately.

Main Phase, Step Two—Meal Suggestions

Meal One and Two

- ❏ Spring Balancing Bowl
- ❏ Cauliflower rice and tahini veggies
- ❏ Wild rice and beet salad
- ❏ Mung bean burger with sunflower cheese
- ❏ Spring salad

Snack

- ❏ Celery and avocado or sunflower seed cheese

Recipes for the Calorie Restriction phase

Like the previous suggestions, these recipes can be used as a guide. Feel free to omit or add things to the recipes so they fit your unique needs.

Sample Meal Plan for Main Phase Step 2			
Day	Meal 1	Meal 2	Snack
Day 8	Spring Balancing Bowl	Spring salad	Celery stick with avocado
Day 9	Mung bean flax burger	Cauliflower rice and veggies	Celery stick with sunflower seed cheese
Day 10	Spring Balancing Bowl	Wild rice and beet salad	Celery stick with avocado

DAY 8-10 | LUNCH AND DINNER RECIPES

Spring Balancing Bowl
1-2 Servings

- ½ cup steel cut oats, soaked in 2 cups water
- 1 Tablespoon ghee
- 1 teaspoon cumin seeds
- ½ teaspoon curry powder
- Small amount of fresh ginger, minced
- ½ cup red cabbage, diced
- 1 celery stalk, diced
- 1 cup water

1. Soak steel cut oats overnight in water with a splash of juice from a jar of kraut or inoculum from your soaked grains.
2. Place ghee in a soup pot and add cumin seeds. When the seeds brown or become fragrant, add curry powder and fresh ginger.

3. Add the soaked steel cut oats, cabbage, and celery.
4. Add water, bring to a boil, then turn on low heat for 10-20 minutes. Check consistency and add water when needed.

> **A NOTE ABOUT RED CABBAGE**
>
> Red cabbage is a member of the *Brassicaceae* family, like mustard and broccoli. The color of the cabbage is dependent on the pH balance of the soil it grows in. One of the main reasons red cabbage is such a popular vegetable is the wealth of **phytochemicals**, antioxidants, nutrients, vitamins, and minerals. Components include **B-vitamins**, **calcium**, **manganese**, **magnesium**, **iron**, and **potassium**, as well as **vitamin C**, **vitamin A**, **vitamin E**, and **vitamin K**. Red cabbage has a lot of organic compounds and antioxidants like anthocyanins and indoles. The main ingredient in kraut is cabbage. Although the media focuses on explaining the probiotic benefits of fermented foods, many of the beneficial aspects of kraut are from the cabbage itself. I recommend using red cabbage whenever possible. Here are some of its benefits:
>
> 1. Anticancer potential[70]
> 2. Antiaging properties[71]
> 3. Reducing inflammation and pain in the stomach[72]
> 4. Protects against neurodegenerative disorders
> 5. Improves bone health

DAY 8-10 | LUNCH AND DINNER RECIPES
Cauliflower Rice and Tahini Veggies
4 Servings

Cauliflower Rice

- 1 medium cauliflower
- 1 Tablespoon avocado oil
- 1 Tablespoon lemon juice
- ¼ teaspoon curry powder
- 1 pinch sea salt

Veggies

- ¼ cup of red cabbage
- ¼ cup broccoli
- ¼ cup tahini

1. Use the largest holes on a cheese grater, or use a food processor, to turn the cauliflower into rice shaped pieces.
2. Lightly sauté the rice shaped cauliflower in olive oil for about 5 minutes. Add the lemon juice, curry powder, red cabbage, and salt, then cook another 5 minutes or until tender.
3. Add broccoli and cook for another 5 minutes. Add tahini and serve.

Wild Rice and Beet Salad
4 servings

- ½ cup wild rice
- 2 cups water
- 1 large, grated beet
- 1 cup parsley chopped fine
- 2 Tablespoons Dijon mustard
- ¼ cup balsamic vinegar
- Juice from ½ a lemon
- 2 Tablespoons olive oil
- Salt to taste

DAY 8-10 | LUNCH AND DINNER RECIPES

1. Soak wild rice overnight (or longer) in the inoculum.
2. Place the soaked wild rice in a soup pot, add water, and bring to a boil. Then turn heat to low, cover, and cook for about 20 minutes. (Note: I usually cook wild rice in a pressure cooker.)
3. When most of the water has been absorbed, add the grated beets and cook for another 5-10 minutes.
4. Remove from heat and add parsley.
5. To make the dressing, place the mustard, balsamic vinegar, lemon, and olive oil in a small blender and pulse until emulsified.
6. Add salt to taste and serve.

A NOTE ABOUT BEETS

Beets belong to the *Chenopodiaceae* family, and the earliest signs of their cultivation was approximately 4,000 years ago in the Mediterranean region. They are a good source of vitamins and minerals, such as **potassium**, **sodium**, iron, folate, **phosphorus**, **magnesium**, **calcium**, **vitamin C**, and B vitamins such as thiamin, **niacin**, and **riboflavin**. Rich in antioxidants, beets get their deep color from the betalain pigment. They are also abundant in phytochemical compounds such as anthocyanins, carotenoids, **lutein/zeaxanthin**, glycine, and betaine. You have noticed that many of the recipes in the is book have included beets. This is why. Benefits of beets:

1. Increase oxygen uptake in athletes.[73]
2. Improve digestion.[74]
3. Neuroprotective for the aging brain.
4. Reduce complications of chronic disease.

DAY 8-10 | LUNCH AND DINNER RECIPES

Mung Bean Carrot Burgers
4-6 Servings

- ½ cup dry, whole mung beans
- 3 cups water
- 1 cup grated carrot
- ¼ cup parsley (chopped)
- 1 Tablespoon curry powder
- 1 Tablespoon fenugreek powder
- 1 Tablespoon mustard powder
- 1 Flax "egg" (¼ cup water mixed with 1 heaping Tablespoon ground flax seeds, let sit 10 minutes)
- ¼ cup tapioca flour
- 2 large pinches of pink rock salt

1. Soak mung beans overnight. Drain the water and placed soaked beans and three cups of fresh water in a pressure cooker. Cook on high pressure for about 15 minutes until beans are soft. Drain excess water and let beans cool.
2. Preheat oven to 375 degrees.
3. When cool place the mung beans in a small bowl and mash. Add carrot, spices, salt, and parsley, and mix well.
4. Add the flax egg (make sure the mixture sat for 10 minutes) and mix.
5. Add the tapioca flour, salt, and stir with a spoon until the mix holds together like a dough. (Depending on how much water your mung beans have in them, you may need more flour.)
6. Place on a sheet pan and cook for 20-30 minutes. Remember, the beans are already cooked so this step is really just to meld the ingredients.
7. Serve with sunflower cheese.

DAY 8-10 | LUNCH AND DINNER RECIPES

Raw Cultured Sunflower Cheese
4-6 Servings

- 1 cup raw, unshelled sunflower seeds
- ¼ cup hemp seeds
- ⅓ cup filtered water
- ⅛ teaspoon Himalayan rock salt (pink or white)

1. Soak the sunflower seeds in water (at least an inch to cover) overnight.

2. In the morning, drain the seeds. Add to a high-speed blender with ⅓ cup of water and salt.
3. Place in a jar and close the lid loosely. Leave in a warm place for one to two days. If you live in a warm climate, the countertop is fine. If you live in cooler climates, leave the jar in the oven with the oven light on.
4. After one to two days, stir with a spoon and taste. If you would like it a little tangier, leave it to sit out another day. Always use a fresh spoon when tasting the cheese.
5. When ready, place jar in the fridge with the lid closed. Sunflower seed cheese will last several weeks in the fridge, but will become more tangy/fermented each day!
6. When ready to eat, take out and enjoy! A few drops of lemon juice go very well with the cheese, too.

Spring Salad with Kraut

1-2 Servings

- 1 handful mescaline mix or other salad mix
- ½ cup shredded beet
- 2 Tablespoons kraut
- 1 teaspoon of hemp seeds

Dressing

- ½ cup olive oil
- ½ cup lemon juice
- 1 Tablespoon dijon mustard
- ½ cup parsley
- 1 teaspoon salt

1. Place all salad ingredients on a plate or bowl.
2. Place all dressing ingredients in a blender and pulse for a few seconds to emulsify the oil.
3. Toss all ingredients together.

DAY 8-10 | SNACK RECIPE

Celery and Avocado Snack

1. Cut up some celery and mash up some avocado with salt.
2. Dip the celery in the avocado.

Shopping List for the Main Cleanse Phase, Step Two (includes items from Pantry list)

GRAINS

- ☐ 1 cup organic steel cut oats
- ☐ 1 cup organic wild rice
- ☐ Tapioca flour

BEANS

- ☐ 1 cup whole mung beans

NUTS AND SEEDS

- ☐ 1 jar of organic salted tahini
- ☐ Ground flax seed
- ☐ Sunflower seeds
- ☐ Hemp seeds

OILS AND VINEGAR

- ☐ Organic cultured ghee
- ☐ Extra virgin olive oil
- ☐ Organic avocado oil
- ☐ Organic balsamic vinegar

CONDIMENTS AND OTHER

- ☐ Veggie kraut
- ☐ 1 jar dijon mustard

FRUITS

- ☐ Lemon

DAY 8-10 | SHOPPING LIST

HERBS AND SPICES

- ☐ Cumin seed
- ☐ Curry powder
- ☐ Cumin powder
- ☐ Fenugreek powder
- ☐ Mustard powder
- ☐ 6 inches of fresh ginger
- ☐ salt

VEGETABLES

- ☐ ½ red cabbage
- ☐ 1 head celery
- ☐ 1 medium cauliflower
- ☐ 1 head of broccoli
- ☐ Salad mix
- ☐ 1 red beet
- ☐ kraut
- ☐ 1 bunch green leafy veggies
- ☐ 2 bunches parsley
- ☐ 1 medium sized carrot
- ☐ Celery
- ☐ Avocado

DAY 11–14
Integration Phase (4 days) | GOAL: Rejuvenate

pg 151

pg 153

pg 154

pg 150

> **A note about using the word *rejuvenate*:** *Rejuvenation is very similar in its meaning to restoration which was the last phase. Both words encourage pouring new, fresh energy into something. In the context of this cleanse the restore phase is meant to create a foundation for health and the rejuvenate phase is meant to build the healthy routines onto that foundation.*

Guidelines for the Integration Phase

In the last phase—Repair and Restore—you used a calorie restricted diet to balance the *Kapha* functions of the liver and to encourage the body to clean out additional *Ama* stored in the fat cells. In this phase of the cleanse, you will continue to promote the beneficial functions of *Kapha*. This phase is designed to rejuvenate the colon and the brain.[75] *Kapha* protects and nourishes the brain and spinal cord and is therefore associated with memory. Research has found a link between the microbiome and the nervous system that *Ayurveda* was aware of thousands of years ago.

Physical

The focus of the Rejuvenate phase is on supporting the gut microbiome—the ecosystem of microorganisms—through the consumption of healthy probiotic foods. Probiotic foods containing different strains of live bacteria improve your gut health by adding to the diversity of its microbiome. Thousands of years ago, bacterial imbalances caused by *Krimi* (worms and unhealthy microorganisms) were treated in *Ayurveda* by changing the gut environment and focusing on the health of the digestive tract. This approach is based around the understanding that microorganisms make up 90% of the cells in the body, most of which are found in the large intestine. Today, natural medicine practitioners are treating *Krimi* in a similar way by focusing on healing the gut and increasing the number of beneficial probiotics (live bacteria) residing in it. This approach has only become popular in recent years after the discovery of antibiotics in 1928, when Western scientists discovered there is more to healing the gut than just killing the bad bacteria. *Ayurveda*, however, has been using this knowledge in their treatment methods for millennia.

Probiotics support normal gut transit time (the time it takes for consumed food to pass through the gut), healthy bowel consistency, and normal frequency of bowel movements.[81] The gut microbiome is a dynamic and responsive system and can change in less than three days. You can learn more about this in Appendix II. Changes in the microbiome will support the following functions:

- The production of vitamin K, A, E, D, and B vitamins.
- The activation of polyphenols and antioxidant plant compounds.
- Regulation of metabolism through insulin.
- Positive influence on the body's immunity.
- Positive influence on brain health and mood.[76]

As you can see supporting the microbiome is essential for long term health.

Emotional/Mental

The goal of the Emotional/Mental level of the Rejuvenate phase is to become established in positive thoughts and emotions. In the previous phases you removed the negative *Kapha* emotions with a ritual and identified positive emotions for which you are grateful. To establish and retain positive thoughts and emotions, create affirmations you can repeat throughout the day. This will help you to use all the best qualities of *Kapha* such as consistency, stamina, endurance, and presence. As your mind wanders during the day you can return to the simple affirmation you composed for yourself.

Create something that really resonates with you and will be easy to remember. It might be something like:

> *I love myself and others,*
>
> *I am open and awake,*
>
> *I live life to the fullest.*

Repeat it verbally and in your mind throughout the day. You can create up to three affirmations, but it's best to start with one.

Spiritual

In the last phase you restored your commitment to the practices that facilitate connection with spirit. With this "inner-compass tune up," it's time to rejuvenate your connection with spirit, itself. If *Kapha* is out of balance, spiritual practice often feels like a chore.

In order to rejuvenate your spiritual life, include trying on new practices. Often the novelty of doing something new can help break the cycle of routine, leading you from habit and into dynamic practice. Try walking meditations or body centered meditations like yoga. You will know if you are truly rejuvenating your connection because you will feel rejuvenated, peaceful, and capable of connecting more deeply with yourself.

Community

Rejuvenate your connection with community. During these days of the cleanse, ask Where is fresh, new energy needed in your community? How can you offer this new energy into those relationships? If you already leave community events and gatherings feeling alive and radiant, you may not need to do this. However, if you leave community gatherings feeling morose, stuck, and despondent, then it's time to take charge and infuse them with new life—just like the spring infuses life into the cold ground of winter. By *investing* energy and life into your community, you will receive more balanced energy in return, which will feed you in new ways.

Sometimes at social gatherings, we attempt to fill voids of connection with other people through food. But when this happens too much *Kapha* accumulates. Instead, while with other people, focus on how community fills you with joy and happiness. What part of yourself can you bring forward as a generous offering? When you start to infuse new energy into your relationships you will find that they give you the energy you have been trying to get from your food. Your *Ojas* will expand and your balanced *Kapha* will thrive.

Environmental

This is also the time to rejuvenate your connection with the Earth. So far you have been connecting with the planet and the local land on which you live. Now it is time to broaden your vision to see how your actions affect others you do not know. In what ways are you committed to supporting things that are healthy and healing for the planet? I have suggested regenerative agriculture and clean water, but really any larger commitment will do. Brainstorm on a piece of paper what you are passionate about, and then research or talk with people about how these passions can connect with larger issues at play. Anything you can do for a larger scale will make a difference for the planet. It may feel strang to step out of your comfort zone to think this large, but try it. Note what happens with your *Kapha* and your sensations of balance, ground, flexibility, and steadiness.

Integration Phase Specific Recommendation

1. **Physical** – Eat 1-2 Tablespoons of kraut or another fermented food/liquid with every meal.
2. **Emotional/mental** – Pick 3 affirmations based on your gratitude journal and recite them when you wake up and when you fall asleep.
3. **Spiritual** – Commit more of your time and energy to a spiritual life by increasing the amount of time you meditate from 20 minutes to 27 minutes or to find that meditative state throughout your day. Experience how your spiritual practice rejuvenates you.
4. **Community** – Assess how your weekly community commitments make you feel and what it means to be a part of a community. Notice all the ways that community fills you with joy and happiness and how that gives you a sense of belonging. Find one thing you can do to give back to your community or invest in this community.
5. **Environmental** – Pay attention to how the land you live and work on is connected to the larger landscape. Find ways to honor that connection. Maybe that is by creating little altars outside, or by watering a wild tree on your drive home. Expand your care of the environment beyond what directly benefits you.

Integration Phase Meal Suggestions

Breakfast

- ❑ Green smoothie
- ❑ Apple, lime, arugula smoothie
- ❑ Buckwheat crepes with ginger chutney

Lunch and Dinner

- ❑ Spring salad
- ❑ Amaranth Bowl with salsa verde
- ❑ Cauliflower and pistachio salad
- ❑ Mustard marinated kale with asparagus

Recipes for the Integration Phase

Like the previous suggestions these recipes can be used as a guide. Feel free to omit or add things to the recipes so that they fit your unique constitution.

Day	Breakfast	Lunch	Dinner
Day 11	Green smoothie	Spring salad with kraut	Amaranth bowl with salsa verde with kraut
Day 12	Apple lime arugula smoothie	Mustard marinated kale and asparagus	Cauliflower and pistachio salad
Day 13	Buckwheat crepes with ginger chutney	Spring salad with kraut	Amaranth bowl with salsa verde with kraut
Day 14	Green smoothie	Mustard marinated kale and asparagus	Mustard marinated kale and asparagus

DAY 11-14 | KRAUT RECIPE

Kapha Kraut
10-20 Servings

- 1 head of green cabbage, cored and shredded
- ½ medium sized onion, chopped fine
- ¼ cup whole caraway seeds
- ¼ cup minced fresh ginger
- 2 Tablespoons black peppercorns
- 2 Tablespoons salt
- Half gallon hermetically sealed jar
- Small jar that can fit inside the hermetically sealed jar

1. Chop the green cabbage and place in a large bowl.
2. Chop the onion and place on top of the green cabbage.
3. Add caraway seeds, peppercorns, fresh ginger, and salt.
4. Knead all ingredients together with your hands for about five minutes.
5. Stuff the mixture into a clean, dry, hermetically sealed jar, using a spoon to press the kraut down firmly as you go.
6. Place a smaller jar inside the hermetically sealed jar and use the lid to gently press it down so that you can close the hermetically sealed jar.
7. As you seal the hermetically sealed jar it will push the kraut down and allow the liquid to rise above the level of the vegetables.
8. Anything above the water line will usually mold. If there are little bubbles of green mold scoop them off. If there is anything more than that then start over. This is described in detail in Appendix V.
9. Place a plate under the closed jar just in case the liquid spills over. Allow the closed jar to sit and rest for two days if it is hot, or 4 days if it is cold, in your house.
10. Taste the contents. Once you are satisfied, remove the smaller jar and transfer the kraut to the refrigerator. The kraut will be best after two weeks.

Note: most hermetically sealed jars have glass on the inside of the lid. There is also glass at the top of the smaller jar you are placing inside. You want enough pressure to push down the smaller jar, but not so much you run the risk of breaking the jar or the lid.

DAY 11-14 | BREAKFAST RECIPES

Green Smoothie
1 serving

- Two handfuls of spinach
- 16 ounces of room temperature water
- 1 small peeled and deseeded cucumber
- 1 teaspoon lemon juice
- Small handful fresh basil leaves

Blend all ingredients. Drink straightaway.

Apple and Arugula Smoothie
1 serving

- 1 apple, cored
- ½ lemon, juiced
- 2 cups fresh arugula
- 1 teaspoon fresh ginger root, chopped
- 1 cup water

Blend all ingredients. Drink straightaway.

DAY 11-14 | BREAKFAST RECIPES

Buckwheat Crepes with Ginger Chutney
6 Servings

- 1 cup buckwheat, ground
- 1 cup water
- 2 flax "eggs" (½ cup water mixed with 2 heaping Tablespoons ground flax seeds, let sit 10 minutes)
- ½ teaspoon cinnamon
- ¼ teaspoon ginger powder
- Ghee/oil for cooking

1. Mix all ingredients in a bowl. Let mixture sit for 8-10 minutes.
2. When ready to cook, put ghee/oil on a pan on medium heat. Take three Tablespoons of batter and spread thin with the back of a spoon.
3. When bubbles start to appear on the top side, carefully flip crepe and cook other side for a few minutes.

DAY 11–14 | BREAKFAST RECIPES

Ginger Chutney
6 Servings

- 1 ½ cups chopped peeled ginger
- 1 cup raisins, soaked
- 1 Tablespoon lemon juice
- ⅓ cup orange juice
- 1 Tablespoon sea salt

1. Soak raisins overnight. Drain raisin water.
2. Peel ginger with the round end of a spoon. Place the ginger, raisins, lemon juice, orange juice, and salt into a food processor and pulse until chunky.
3. Pack into a glass jar. Make sure ingredients are submerged in liquid, adding more water if necessary. Let sit for two days at room temperature and then transfer to the refrigerator.
4. Use within two months of making.

Note: Crepes are difficult to make and often stick to the pan if the temperature isn't just right. If you don't feel confident in your crepe making abilities, you may want to practice this ahead or skip this recipe.

DAY 11-14 | LUNCH AND DINNER RECIPES

Spring Salad with Kraut
1 Serving

- 1 handful mescalin mix
- ½ cup shredded beet
- 1 cup broccoli sprouts

Dressing

- ½ cup olive oil
- ½ cup lemon juice
- ½ cup parsley
- 1 teaspoon salt

To make the dressing, whisk together in a bowl with a fork, shake together in a jar, or blend together in a blender. Drizzle over the salad and enjoy.

DAY 11-14 | LUNCH AND DINNER RECIPES

Amaranth Bowl with Salsa Verde and Kraut
2 Servings

- 1 ½ cups of water
- ½ cup of amaranth

1. Soak *Amaranth* overnight in inoculum and water.
2. Drain the water from the soaked *Amaranth*.
3. Boil water in a soup pot. Place the soaked *Amaranth* into the water. Return to a boil and reduce heat. Cook for about 20 minutes or until the water is absorbed.

Salsa Verde

- ½ cup fresh parsley leaves
- ½ cup fresh basil leaves
- 1 small jalapeno, deseeded
- 2 teaspoons lemon juice
- 2 teaspoons apple cider vinegar
- ½ cup of olive oil
- 1 Tablespoon nutritional yeast
- ¼ teaspoon salt
- 1 pinch cumin

1. Mix all ingredients in a food processor or blender and blend until smooth. You may have to add water to get the right consistency. The salsa verde will keep, tightly covered, in the refrigerator for up to three days.
2. Mix with the *Amaranth*. Top with kraut and broccoli sprouts and serve.

DAY 11-14 | LUNCH AND DINNER RECIPES

Cauliflower and Pistachio Salad
4 Servings

- 1 large cauliflower
- 1 cup yellow onion, roughly sliced
- 5 Tablespoons olive oil
- Salt
- 1 cup parsley, roughly chopped
- ½ cup mint, roughly chopped
- ½ cup tarragon, roughly chopped
- ½ cup shelled pistachios, lightly toasted and chopped
- 1 teaspoon cumin
- ⅓ teaspoon lemon juice

1. Preheat oven to 425 degrees.
2. Coarsely chop a third of the cauliflower into florets, roughly one to two inches wide, and add these to a separate bowl with the cauliflower leaves, if you have any, and the onion. Toss everything together with two Tablespoons of oil and ¼ teaspoon of salt, then spread out on a large parchment-lined baking sheet. Roast for about 20 minutes, until cooked through and golden brown. Remove from the oven and set aside to cool.
3. Once cool, put the roasted vegetables into a large bowl with 3 Tablespoons oil, the grated cauliflower, and parsley, mint, tarragon, pistachios, cumin and lemon juice, along with ¼ teaspoon salt. Toss gently, just to combine, then transfer to a bowl and serve.

Mustard Marinated Kale with Asparagus
4 Servings

- 3 Tablespoons toasted pumpkin seeds
- 1 bunch kale, destemmed
- 3 Tablespoons olive oil
- ½ teaspoon apple cider vinegar
- 2 teaspoons dijon mustard
- 1 bunch asparagus, woody ends trimmed off
- ½ cup tarragon leaves
- ½ cup fresh dill, roughly chopped, or 2 Tablespoons dry dill

1. Preheat the oven to 350 degrees.
2. Mix the pumpkin seeds with ⅛ teaspoon of salt and a little black pepper. Spread across a small parchment-lined baking sheet and bake for two minutes until the seeds are golden brown. Set aside for about 30 minutes; the seeds will stick together as they cool and crisp up, but can be broken into small pieces.
3. Put the kale into a large bowl with two Tablespoons of the oil, the vinegar, mustard, and ¼ teaspoon of salt. Mix together well, using your hands to massage the kale for about one minute, until it softens and takes on the flavors of the marinade. Set aside for 30 minutes or longer.
4. Put the remaining one Tablespoon of oil into large frying pan and place over medium high heat. Add asparagus and ⅛ teaspoon of salt and fry for six minutes, turning over throughout the cooking process so all sides start to brown and soften. Set aside to cool, then slice on an angle into one-inch pieces.
5. When ready to serve, add the asparagus, tarragon, and dill to the kale and mix well. Spread out on the large platter, sprinkle with seeds, and serve.

DAY 11-14 | SHOPPING LIST

Shopping List for the Integration Phase (includes items from Pantry list)

GRAINS

- ☐ Buckwheat
- ☐ Amaranth

NUTS AND SEEDS

- ☐ Ground flax seed
- ☐ 1 cup sunflower seeds
- ☐ 1 cup shelled pistachios
- ☐ 1 cup pumpkin seeds

OILS

- ☐ Organic grass-fed cultured ghee
- ☐ Organic extra virgin olive oil

CONDIMENTS AND OTHER

- ☐ Apple cider vinegar
- ☐ Dijon mustard
- ☐ Nutritional yeast

FRUITS

- ☐ 3-5 lemons
- ☐ 1-3 apples
- ☐ 1 cup raisins
- ☐ 1 pint orange juice

HERBS AND SPICES

- ☐ 10 inches of fresh ginger
- ☐ Black peppercorns
- ☐ Cumin powder
- ☐ Salt
- ☐ Caraway seeds

DAY 11-14 | SHOPPING LIST

VEGETABLES

- ☐ 1 large green cabbage
- ☐ 1 bunch spinach or other leafy greens
- ☐ 1 cucumber
- ☐ 1 bunch basil
- ☐ 1 bunch arugula
- ☐ Mescalin salad mix
- ☐ 1 red beet
- ☐ Broccoli sprouts
- ☐ 2 bunches of parsley
- ☐ 1 jalapeno
- ☐ 1 large cauliflower
- ☐ 1 medium yellow onion
- ☐ 1 bunch parsley
- ☐ 1 bunch mint
- ☐ 1 bunch tarragon
- ☐ 1 bunch kale
- ☐ 1 bunch asparagus
- ☐ 1 bunch dill

Part IV: Completion

After the Spring Ayurvedic Cleanse Program

Congratulations! You have completed the Spring Ayurvedic Cleanse program. Now it's time to celebrate. Get a massage, throw a party, and treat your friends to a meal with one of the recipes you learned. Do something that will support the sense of accomplishment you feel. Also, remember this is a seasonal diet, so depending on when you started the program, you can keep eating this way for the rest of the season.

You may continue to eat light for some time, decide to maintain your time-restricted feeding, or continue eating *Kichari*. Recognize which new practices you enjoyed the most and continue supporting them. One significant change is all you need, but feel free to adopt more if you're inclined.

A helpful point to remember is that each person is uniquely different. Listen to your body, follow its wisdom, and do your best to learn how to discern between a true bodily need and an impulse that stems from a habit (e.g., eating sweets when you are stressed). The practice of going with your embodied intuition greatly helps because it cuts through the noise of the mind.

Rasayana to Nourish the Body and Mind

At the end of a traditional *Ayurvedic Pancha karma* cleanse, people proceed into *Rasayana*. *Rasayana* is an *Ayurvedic* practice used to replenish the vital energy of the body from a cellular level, starting with the lymphatic fluid. The *Rasayana* process replenishes the body's vital reserves and makes the body and mind resilient. The word itself is composed of the root words "*rasa*" and "*ayana.*" *Rasa* is defined as lymph, emotion, taste, juice, plasma, water, nutrient fluid, and satisfaction, while *ayana* means special study. Lymph in both *Ayurveda* and modern medicine is considered the body's primary means of detoxification and is something that governs immunity.

While *Ayurvedic* cleansing is important, cleanses are used for purifying the system in order to effectively receive the *Rasayana*. At the end of many heroic cleanse programs, I find most people can't wait to jump back into their old eating patterns, and in so doing drive residual toxins *deeper* into their bodies. Therefore, I recommend you do 14 days of *Rasayana* after the Spring Ayurvedic Cleanse in order to replenish your body with strength and vitality.

Rasayana is done after a cleanse when the body and mind are feeling light but also grounded. Removing toxicity from the system allows us to improve cellular nutrition and re-invigorate the intelligence of the body. Another definition of *Rasayana* is "path of essence"—a cleanse is like creating a blank canvas, while rejuvenation is like adding the colors and paint that will turn the canvas into a masterpiece.

Where cleansing focuses on light foods that are easy to digest, *Rasayana* introduces your body to foods that are tonifying and building to the body and mind. I will introduce you to the herbs and foods most often used in *Rasayana*. I also highly recommend you check out Appendix VI, in which I share about the lymphatic system, and how it connects with both *Rasayana* and the *Kapha dosha*.

Rasayana Herbs

Rasayana herbs are tonifying, adaptogenic, and supportive of the entire body. Choose a formula that includes some of the following herbs:

- **Ashwagandha:** This herb helps you adapt to physical and emotional stress and is considered an adaptogen. It helps to reduce inflammation in the digestives system, nervous system, and joints and is considered anti-inflammatory. It helps your body reduce damage caused by free radicals and oxidative stress which are the leading cause of aging, this makes it antioxidant. It supports the bodies detox pathways which makes it antitumor. It can calm or stimulate the nervous system depending on what is needed making it a nervine.

- **Shatavari:** This herb helps you adapt to physical and emotional stress and is considered an adaptogen. It helps your body combat unhelpful bacteria and so it is antibacterial. Cramping that is accompanied by PMS or digestive bloating can be alleviated with this herb making it antispasmodic. It improves your sexual function and vitality making it an aphrodisiac. It is protective of mucus membranes like those in the nose and digestive system which makes it demulcent and gastroprotective. It supports healthy immune function especially of the lungs which makes it a immune tonic, lung tonic. It can be also be helpful for lactating women who are not producing enough milk, this makes it a galactagogue.

- **Amalaki:** This herb is also an adaptogen (are you sensing a trend?) It helps to reduce inflammation in all parts of the body as an anti-inflammatory. It also prevents the oxidative damage associated with aging as an antioxidant. It is protective against all viruses, especially those that cause the common cold. It can help the body to eliminate toxins by promoting normal bowel movements.

- **Schisandra:** This herb is also an adaptogen, antioxidant, and anti-inflammatory like many of the preceding herbs. It helps support healthy immune function as an immune tonic. It also protects the liver which is used to help the body detoxify and heal, this makes it hepatoprotective. It is also really good for the brain and is a nervine.

- **Tulsi:** This herb is also an adaptogen and antioxidant. It can be used to protect the body against harmful bacteria and viruses as an antibacterial and antiviral. It has been used to support the mind and emotions as an antidepressant. It helps to promote a healthy immune response as an immunomodulator.

- **Astragalus:** This herb is also an adaptogen, antioxidant, and antibacterial. It helps protect the liver as a hepatoprotective. It is used to give strength to the heart as a heart tonic. It is also an immune tonic.

- **Guduchi:** This herb is an adaptogen, anti-inflammatory, antioxidant, hepatoprotective, immune tonic.

- **Licorice:** adaptogen, antiviral, anti-inflammatory, antioxidant, hepatoprotective, and immunomodulator.

Rasayana Foods

In addition to taking Rasayana herbs, meat soup is commonly recommended. The nutrient density of meat makes it remarkable for nourishing the body. But seeing as it is higher on the food chain, it also has a high concentration of chemicals accumulated from the air, soil, and water. For this reason, the best meat sources are wild game meats, but free-range organic meat is fine too. Making stock with the bones of these animals is the best way to get the nutrition from meat without compromising digestion.

- **Wild game meats:** venison, elk, caribou, and moose
- **Wild cold-water fish:** salmon, pike, char, sardines, smelt, herring
- **Pasture-raised poultry:** chicken, duck, turkey, and pheasant
- **Free-range meats:** lamb, sheep, goat, and bison

If your digestion is powerful enough to digest these highly nutritive foods and herbs, the following 14 days after the Spring Cleanse is a good time to eat them, as they tone and nourish your body.

Rasayana Lifestyle Practices

Rasayana is like cleansing, in that it requires us to slow down and redirect some of our energy towards self-repair. Instead of using our energy to accomplish external tasks, we use some for internal activities. Some practices beneficial for rejuvenation are:

- Daily *Abhyanga* (oil massage)
- Slowing down and resting more
- Spending less time on computers and mobile phones
- Gentle exercise

Cultivating vitality and internal strength allows us to fill our tanks so we can walk our paths in life with ease. Taking time to rejuvenate will also make us more resilient to disease.

For 14 days after the cleanse, slow down, spend extra time in nature, and enjoy the bodily sensations you experience from gentle exercise.

Reintroduction of your favorite foods

After finishing the cleanse and the *Rasayana* mentioned above, it is time to start reintroducing new types of foods. This is where most people run into trouble, either eating too much, too complex, or to many types of foods all at once. The tendency is to go out and binge on the foods you have been restricting. I hope the *Rasayana* section has provided the mental fortitude to moderate the foods you reintroduce. Your body is clean and may be very sensitive to rich foods, so take your explorations slowly so you can track the effects of these foods on your body. You will now have instant feedback about which foods support your body and which ones do not.

I recommend doing a specific process for this reintroduction. Write down the five foods you would like to reintroduce, such as:

1. Chicken
2. Yogurt
3. Green tea
4. Eggs
5. Wine

Once you have a list, introduce the first food, in this case chicken, then wait three days before introducing yogurt. Wait another three days before introducing green tea, and onward. This gives your body time to adjust to the new food. Sometimes you will find your body has a hard time digesting a food you used to eat. Reintroduce this food in smaller amounts over a longer period of time, allowing your body to acclimate, and consider reducing the amount of this food you eat to support your long-term digestive capacity. After 15 days (if everything goes smoothly) you will have introduced all five foods on your list. Create a new list and keep going.

Based on this feedback, you can go forward and make conscious choices that will support you in health and wellness rather than being confused about what is or is not working for you. This sensitivity may also mean you can no longer eat unconsciously. Some of the foods or dietary practices you enjoyed prior to the program may now make you feel sick; take time to process your grief around releasing these old comforts.

Conclusion

You have just spent the last 14 days following the recommendations and instructions of this program, possibly 14 days in *Rasayana*, and an additional 15–30 days reintroducing foods. You have:

- Learned some basic principles of Ayurveda,
- Given thought to how you prepare and eat foods,
- Tried new foods and different ways of creating meals,
- Added new self-care practices to your daily routine,
- And, most importantly, you have spent time taking care of yourself and tending to your health and wellness

The most common question I hear at the end of a program is, "What do I do now?" I have been holding your hand through the entire process and telling you exactly what to do, and now it is possible you feel like you are on your own. Thankfully that is not true!

Make a list of everything you have learned. Document what was easy for you, what was enjoyable, what was challenging, and what you never want to try again. Do that now; it will only take five to ten minutes.

With your newly collected information, commit to continuing the practices you enjoyed. Give yourself one to two weeks to slowly go back to your life prior to the program and stay attentive to what happens.

This is a great time to go on a yoga or mediation retreat or do other activities that require a pure and clear mind. Instead of looking at this as the end of the program, look at it as the beginning of a new you.

I would like to express my sincere gratitude for your commitment to this program. I have been following and leading similar *Ayurvedically*-inspired programs since 2008, and I understand the amount of effort and energy you have devoted. It is an honor to share this wisdom with you, and I look forward to continuing to support your vibrant health using *Ayurvedic* principles.

Note: Please don't hesitate to contact me at www.rhythmofhealing.com if you have ideas or suggestions on how this program and manual can be improved.

Appendix I: Constitutional Questionnaire

Mental

	Vata	**Pitta**	**Kapha**
Mental activity	Quick mind, restless	Sharp intellect, aggressive	Calm, steady stable
Memory	Good Short term	Good overall	Good long term
Thoughts	Always changing	Generally steady	Steady, stable, fixed
Concentration	Good Short term	Better than average	Good ability for long term focus
Ability to learn	Quick grasp	Medium grasp	Slow grasp
Dreams	Fearful, flying	Angry, adventurous	Water, relationships
Sleep	Interrupted, light	Sound medium	Sound, heavy, long
Voice	High pitch	Medium pitch	Low pitch
TOTAL			

Behaviorial

	Vata	**Pitta**	**Kapha**
Eating speed	Quick	Medium	Slow
Hunger level	Irregular	Needs food when hungry	Can easily miss meals
Food & drink	Prefers warm	Prefers cold	Prefers dry and warm
Sharing & giving	Gives a little	Large, infrequent giving	Gives generously
Works best	While supervised	Alone	In groups
Weather preference	Aversion to cold	Aversion to heat	Aversion to damp, cold
Reaction to stress	Excites quickly	Medium	Slow to get excited
Piggy bank	Doesn't save, spends quickly	Saves, big spender	Saves regularly, accumulates wealth
Friendships	Makes friends easily, short term friends	Tends to be a loner, friends often family members	Forms long lasting friendships
TOTAL			

Emotional

	Vata	*Pitta*	*Kapha*
Reacts to stress with	Fear	Anger, memory	Indifference
Sensitive to	Own feelings	Not sensitive	Other's feelings
If threatened, tends to	Run	Fight	Make peace
Relations with parents	Clingy	Jealous	Secure
Expresses affection	With words	With actions	With touch
When feeling hurt	Cries	Argues	Withdraws
Emotional trauma causes	Anxiety	Anger	Depression
Confidence level	Timid	Outwardly self-confident	Inner confidence
TOTAL			

Physical

	Vata	*Pitta*	*Kapha*
Hair amount	Thin	Average	Thick
Hair type	Dry	Normal	Oily
Hair color	Light brown, blond	Red, auburn	Dark brown, black
Skin	Dry, rough	Soft medium	Oily, moist cool
Skin temperature	Cold hands/feet	Warm	Cool
Complexion	Darker	Pink-red	Pale-white
Eyes	Small	Medium	Large
Whites of eyes	Blue/brown	Yellow/red	White/glossy
Size of teeth	Very large/small	Small-medium	Medium-large
Weight	Thin, hard to gain	Medium	Heavy, gains easily
Elimination	Dry, hard, thin, easily constipated	Many during day, soft to normal	Heavy, slow, thick, regular
TOTAL			

Fitness

	Vata	*Pitta*	*Kapha*
Exercise tolerance	Low	Medium	High
Endurance	Fair	Good	Excellent
Strength	Fair	Good	Excellent
Speed	Very good	Good	Not so fast
Competition	Doesn't like pressure to compete	Driven, competitive	Deals easily with pressure to compete
Walking speed	Fast	Average	Slow and steady
Muscle tone	Slim	Average	Brawny
Runs like	Deer	Tiger	Bear
Body size	Small frame, lean or long	Medium frame	Large frame, fleshy
Reaction time	Quick	Average	Slow

Fitness total

TOTALS

	Vata	*Pitta*	*Kapha*
Mental			
Behavioral			
Emotional			
Physical			
Fitness			
Type			

General Recommendations for *Kapha*

To Balance *Kapha* in the Spring

- *Be Active*
- Stimulating activities
- Physical labor
- Stay warm, stay active
- Sunbathing
- No naps
- Mix it up (variety of activities)
- Avoid cold and damp
- Cultivate physical challenges
- Mental stimulation
- Travel
- Avoid "couch potato" behavior

Life Force Enhancing Exercises:

1. Walk barefoot on the earth for 10 minutes every day. Intend to absorb nourishment from the Earth.
2. Walk along natural bodies of water. Allow the fluid influence of water to infuse you.
3. Allow the light and warmth of the sun to permeate you.
4. Take a walk where there is abundant vegetation and deeply inhale the breath of the plants.
5. Gaze into the heavens at night. Allow your awareness to touch the stars and the furthest reaches of the cosmos.

Appendix II: Fermented Cereals and Legumes

Most traditional agricultural societies have a long history of processing cereals and legumes using fermentation. Examples are the sourdough breads of Europe, chocolate (from cacao, Central America), ogi (from sorghum, West Africa), injera (from teff, East Africa), idli (from rice and urad, South India), and natto (from soy, Japan). This was done to make these cereal grains and legumes more digestible.

There are two basic methods for fermenting cereals and legumes. The first method is too half-cook the grain or legume. Start with the same proportions of water and grain/legume you would normally use for cooking. Cook the grain/legume for half as much time as usual. Add ¼-cup of brine or leftover live-culture pickle juice; this is called an *inoculant* as it will start to ferment the grain/bean. I usually leave everything in the pot and close the lid. Place the grain in a warm place for up to a week and watch it carefully. You will know it is ready when it starts to smell slightly sour. Fermented grains and legumes can take a couple weeks before they are ready.

The second method is to ferment the grains/legumes before cooking. This is my preferred method because it takes less time and the flavor is less sour. Like sourdough bread, this method begins with a starter.

To make the starter, soak the grain/legume in water for 24 hours in the warmest place in your house. The optimal temperature is 86°F/30°C, though cooler temperatures will still work if you don't want to put your starter in the oven on low heat. Before cooking the grain/bean, reserve a cup of the soaking liquid—this will become the culture for the next soaking batch. Keep repeating the process with fresh ingredients, always retaining one cup of soaking liquid for the next batch. Over time the inoculum will get stronger. After the fourth time you will have an inoculum that can reduce anti-nutrient factors (or ANF's—described in more detail below), such as lectins, by 95%.[77] *If you need to take a break, the inoculum can refrigerate for a week before it dies.*

Fermentation not only boosts the health benefits of grains and beans, but it also reduces lectins in plants such as wheat, grains, and beans.[29] Lectins are plant proteins that bind sugar in plants. As research on lectins develops it has become important for vegetarians and individuals with a plant-based diet to know how to limit the number of lectins in their diets. Most of what we know about lectins has been popularized in Dr. Steven Gundry's book, *The Plant Paradox: The Hidden Dangers in 'Healthy' Foods That Cause Disease and Weight Gain* and by Todd Caldecott's book *Food as Medicine*. Lectins can cause leaky gut and imbalances in the microbiome. A well-known lectin is wheat germ agglutinin (WGA), found in wheat and other seeds in the grass family.[78]

Many lectins are proinflammatory (increases inflammation), immunotoxic (kills immune cells), neurotoxic (kills nerve cells), and cytotoxic (kills cells). Certain lectins may also increase blood viscosity (thicken blood), interfere with gene expression (hinder DNA), and disrupt endocrine (hormone) function.

Wheat fermentation, like sourdough, will reduce the gliadin content in bread. True sourdough requires the strain *Lactobacillus sanfranciscensis* to be fermented for up to 72 hours at 37°C. (Most bakeries don't do this and still call their bread sourdough.) Other examples of fermentation are beet borsht and dairy products (e.g. yogurt).

Oversee your bacteria by controlling what you eat. This is the most efficient way to maintain a healthy microbiome. Eat a diet high in plant fiber, otherwise your only option may be a fecal transplant—don't let it get to that! Focus on digestion and how to improve it.

Pressure cooking can preserve nutrients and neutralize plant lectins when used to cook beans, legumes, and other lectin-containing vegetables. Research has shown the phytic acid—a common lectin—in beans cooked in a pressure cooker was reduced in half, as opposed to beans cooked regularly.

Phytic acid is one of many antinutrient factors (ANFs). They are called ANF's because they take vital minerals from the body in order to be digested. They are also really hard to digest and can lead to gas and bloating. ANF's are extremely common in cereal grains and legumes, and contain proteins such as gliadin (in wheat) and vicilin (in lentils). These proteins are protease inhibitors, meaning they promote gut inflammation by blocking protein-digesting enzymes and provoking autoimmune diseases. These ANF's are how cereals, legumes, or nuts discourage predation by animals. Grasslands all over the world are a testament to how effective grass seed resists mammalian digestion. That is why fermentation emerged to increase the digestibility and nutrient absorption of beans and grains.[80]

The problem with recommending an altogether lectin-free diet is that it would eliminate most plant foods, which should ideally make up the bulk of your diet. Moreover, in small amounts, some lectins can be quite beneficial, so 100-percent avoidance is likely neither possible nor ideal. The key then becomes finding a happy medium where the worst lectins are avoided, and the effect of others are tempered through proper preparation and cooking.

Appendix III: Dry Skin Brushing with Silk Gloves - Garshana

Garshana is a traditional *Ayurvedic* dry massage that stimulates the skin and lymphatic system, done with natural silk gloves, a soft sponge, or a dry brush. The skin's health is supported by the lymphatic system. The lymphatics are vessels in the body that carry white blood cells. These vessels don't have a pump connected to the heart like the arteries, so they depend on movement. This can be exercise or it can be massaging the skin with silk gloves, which supports the natural movement of the lymphatic system.

For more information on the lymphatic system see Appendix VI.

How to Dry Brush

1. Use raw silk gloves or an all-natural body brush.
2. Do this before you shower or bath.
3. Because it can release dry skin you will want to step into the tub or shower.
4. Direct brushing movements towards the heart with long strokes over the limbs and circular movements over the joints and abdomen. Repeat each stroke 5-10 times before moving on to the next.
5. Start at your feet, move in long fluid motions from toes to heel.
6. Then brush from the ankles to the knees. Circle around the knees.
7. Then go from the knees to the hips. Move around the hips in large circular motions.
8. Move in a clockwise motion around your abdomen and be gentle across the chest.
9. For the arms, start at the hands and move in toward the elbows and up to the shoulders and neck.
10. Avoid using the dry brush on your face. Instead use a separate tool made for the sensitive facial skin.

During the program it is best to do this seven days a week, however you can do it as few as three days a week.

- Here are a few suggestions for brushes and gloves:
    - ecotools.com/dry-body-brush/p/7425
    - www.mapi.com/products/massage-oils/silk-massage-gloves.html

Your dry brush or silk gloves should not hurt or be overly rough.

Different than *Abhyanga*

Many people are familiar with the *Ayurvedic* massage called *Abhyanga*, and although the procedure is similar, the effects are different. *Garshana* is more stimulating where *abhyanga* is calming. You can do both procedures if you have the time and interest. They complement each other well.

The Result

Consistent use of *Garshana* can lead to a feeling of vitality and energy. This is due to the positive effect on the lymphatic system and the mobilization of *Ama* out of the body.

Benefits of Dry Skin Brushing

- **Exfoliates the skin.** This not only encourages detoxification, but also leaves you with smooth skin.[81]
- **Enhances lymphatic drainage.** Congestion of your lymphatic system can lead to a host of health problems including inflammation and congestion.[82]
- **Unclogs congested pores.** Dry brushing allows the pores to breathe and prevents toxic build-up.[83]
- **Reduces cellulite.** Cellulite is simply an accumulation of toxic buildup in your fat cells. Dry brushing dislodges the toxins and allows for movement through the various systems of elimination.[84,85,86]
- **Stress relief.** Dry skin brushing can be a form of meditation. It can also soothe the nerves, reduce muscle tension, and calm the mind.[87]

Appendix IV: Growing Broccoli Sprouts

If you've ever heard of sulforaphane, you've probably heard about broccoli sprouts and why they are one of the healthiest foods on the planet. Based on what we know about sulforaphane these sprouts need to be a big part of your spring meals. Here are some of the benefits:

- Helps protect against cancers[88]
- Benefits the heart[89]
- Boosts the brain[90,91,92,93,94,95],
- Increases glutathione[96,97]
- Supports natural detoxification[98,99]

By the time a broccoli sprout becomes broccoli it has less sulforphane, and if you cook broccoli the levels of sulforaphane are reduced even more. Cruciferous vegetables, like broccoli, have many benefits; studies find that eating them a few times a week may reduce your cancer risk by 30% or more. But even this is a small advantage in comparison to broccoli sprouts. The reason to make your own broccoli sprouts is that sulforaphane is at its highest on the fourth day. After the fourth day, the sulforaphane levels decreases. Most store-bought sprouts are much older than four days, so the benefits are lost. Since making your own is really easy, I highly recommend this addition to your diet.

You will need the following supplies:

- Broccoli Seeds: Buy 1 lb or more. I get mine from Food to Live
- Quart (best size) or half-gallon **wide-mouth mason jars.**
- **Wire sprouting lids for the mason jars**
- **Sprouting jar holders** (optional) or a glass bowl that can hold up the jar. Or a bread pan. Get creative.

Broccoli Sprouts Growing Instructions

1. Add two Tablespoons of broccoli seeds, such as Food to Live Organic Broccoli Seeds, to a wide-mouthed glass quart jar. Cover with a few inches of filtered water and cap with the sprouting lid. Store in a warm, dark place overnight.
2. The next morning (or at least 8 hours later), drain off the water and rinse with fresh water.
3. Place the sprouting jar upside down at a 45-degree angle on a sprouting jar stand. Place in warm, dark place.
4. Rinse and drain the sprouts in the morning and evening, placing them back in the jar holder after each rinse. Don't forget, not rinsing your sprouts can lead them to grow bacteria. After a few days the seeds will break open. After about 5 days the sprouts will be about an inch long.
5. Now place the seeds in the sunlight until the leaves become dark green. Once dark green, the sprouts are ready to eat. The whole process takes a week.
6. Wait about 12 hours from the final rinse, so all remaining moisture has drained from the sprouts. Replace the sprouting lids with regular mason jar lids and store in the refrigerator. Try to eat all of them in the first 3-4 days.

Additional Health Benefits of Sulforaphane

One of the reasons sulforaphane is so powerful is that it can cross the blood-brain barrier. This allows it to induce the activity of enzymes that have neuroprotective (protects the brain) effects. Sulforaphane has been studied in neurodevelopmental disorders such as autism. Results found that children with autism had improved social interaction and verbal communication when taking sulfurophane.[139] Broccoli sprout extract reverses biochemical abnormalities, including oxidative stress, decreased antioxidant levels, depressed glutathione synthesis, reduced mitochondrial function, increased lipid peroxidation, and neuroinflammation.[100]

Another neuroprotective effect was found in individuals with traumatic brain injuries (TBI) or concussions. After a concussion there is a lot of oxidative stress and brain inflammation. Broccoli sprout extract was found to upregulate antioxidant pathways and prevent neurotoxicity.[141-143] It is no surprise, then, that broccoli sprouts may be useful for Alzheimer's and Parkinson's disease. In an animal model of Parkinson's disease, sulforaphane was found to inhibit the loss of dopaminergic neurons, or the neurons responsible for the slow movements and shuffling gait. Sulforaphane also protects against amyloid-beta-induced neuronal death in Alzheimer's disease, thus helping to preserve brain function.[101]

We are all exposed to toxins in our water, air, food, and cosmetics. Broccoli sprouts were found to assist Phase 2 liver detoxification, which is responsible for converting toxic metabolites into less toxic compounds that can be excreted by the body. The digestion of broccoli sprouts increases glutathione, the body's master antioxidant and detoxifier, and promotes the rapid and sustained detoxification of environmental pollutants, such as benzene and acrolein. Finally, sulforaphane also decreases the liver enzymes ALT, ALP, and gamma-GTP, indicating that it reduces stress on the liver and restores healthy liver function.

Broccoli sprouts also help our body fight off pathogens. It inhibits the growth of *Helicobacter pylori*, a bacterium that contributes to the development of peptic ulcers.[102] It is also effective against *E. coli*, another gastrointestinal pathogen; *Pseudomonas aeruginosa*, a nosocomial pathogen found in hospitals; and *Staphylococcus aureus*, a bacterium implicated in skin infections.[103] Sprouts even help if the body starts attacking itself, like in autoimmunity. This attack is usually from pro-inflammatory cytokines and autoreactive immune cells.[152] Broccoli sprouts suppress this activity. They can also be used to activate natural killer cells to clear the body of the influenza virus.[104] They boost T helper 1 (Th1) immunity and reverse the decrease in immunity that occurs with aging.[154]

On the subject of inflammation, chronic inflammation is an underlying cause of obesity and metabolic disturbances. It plays a role in insulin resistance and non-alcoholic fatty liver disease. A recent study found that glucoraphanin, the precursor to sulforaphane, mitigates obesity through several mechanisms: it increases mitochondrial biogenesis (production of the cells powerhouse) in fat tissue, thereby increasing metabolic function; improves glucose tolerance and insulin sensitivity; and decreases levels of a pro-inflammatory bacterium (*Desulfovibrionaceae*). All this can be used to combat the metabolic dysfunction causing obesity.

There are many more benefits to broccoli sprouts still not listed here! I hope that you are convinced to make this a part of your spring cleanse, and diet throughout the year.

Note: The exact dosage depends on your needs and your body weight, but in general it is recommended to eat 100g a day, which is about 10 Tablespoons or 3 ounces. Enjoy!

Appendix V: Fermentation – Making Your Own Kraut

Fermentation is achieved either by using a starter culture or creating an environment for wild fermentation to take place. A starter culture is a substance containing the beneficial bacteria we want to colonize which leads to further proliferation. A wild fermentation occurs when an environment is created where the beneficial bacteria already present on the produce can thrive. There are many different types of starter cultures that can be used, including kefir grains, kombucha, jun, and whey. Wild ferments are usually made with a saltwater brine, which allows the naturally occurring probiotics on the produce to proliferate within the environment created by the salt. I will focus on wild fermentation here.

Basics of Fermentation

Fermentation may take some slightly different tools than normal cooking, but you probably have everything you need. Common equipment includes:

- A knife, grater or slicer
- A blunt meat pounder, potato masher, or strong hands
- A large bowl
- Sea salt
- Filtered water
- A fermentation vessel (half gallon mason jar or ceramic crock)

Most likely the only thing you don't have is a fermentation vessel. The basic requirements of a vessel are a cylindrical shape made of glass or ceramics. Square containers can harbor bacteria in the corners, and plastic or metal containers leach chemicals into the kraut. The most common vessels are:

- Canning jars or hermetically latched jars – these are cheap, readily available, and require a certain amount of creativity when weighing down and covering the vegetables.

- Ceramic fermenting crocks – These include everything upon purchase and are made with lead-free clay. If you get one used, make sure it doesn't have any cracks where bacteria can grow.

- Ceramic insert for a slow cooker – The round ones work better than oval ones when creating a weight and covering system.

- Glass jars with an airlock system – These are commonly used for the fermentation of wine or beer. An airlock system allows gas to escape from the jar while sealing oxygen in.

How to Prepare a Ferment

The basic procedure is to lightly wash and cut up the veggies. It is important to use fresh organic produce. Mix the vegetables with sea salt and herbs or spices, then pound or massage the mixture to release the juices. Places the veggies and liquid they released into a jar or fermentation crock and pack tightly until the vegetables are submerged in their own liquids. A weight can be used to press the veggies below the water line and keep them from being exposed to air where they can grow mold. I like to use a hermetically latched jar and a smaller jar that pushes the veggies down under the water line. Also make sure the water line is an inch below the top of the jar as the jar will release air—and sometimes liquid if the water line is too close to the top. The best temperature for lacto-fermentation to occur is about 72 degrees. The best environment is a dry, dark place. It can take up to six weeks for full fermentation to occur.

Monitoring Your Ferment for Readiness

Fermentation depends on temperature. The warmer the environment in which the ferment takes place, the faster the ferment occurs. Keep an eye out for the signs the vegetables are ready to transfer to the refrigerator:

- Bubbles will form in the jar. As fermentation progresses the *Lactobacilli* bacteria create gases as they break down the starches and sugars in the vegetables.

- The vegetables will smell sour. If they smell rotten, nasty, or putrid then it is time to start over.

- If it has passed both previous two tests, then give it a taste. The flavor will be sour. When your ferment has a flavor reminiscent of sauerkraut it is time to move it into cold storage. Also note that flavors will change over time. I recommend tasting the ferment once a week; once you find the flavor you like, put the jar in the refrigerator to slow the fermentation process. In warmer environments this process takes about 4 weeks and in colder environments it can take up to 6 weeks.

Identifying Possible Problems with Your Ferment

True mold comes in round, colorful deposits, although some molds are white. Molds and yeasts require oxygen to grow which is why it is best to have a lid on your ferment and to have all the produce under liquid. If mold develops, scrape off the mold and any veggies that it might have touched. To avoid mold, use the recommended amount of salt and fresh vegetables, make sure the vegetables are submerged, and ferment your veggies as close to 72 degrees as possible.

Foamy Brine

The brine may become foamy depending on the type of vegetables used. Vegetables with higher sugar content, like beets, may foam the most. A little bit of foam is fine, but too much means something has gone wrong.

Pungent odor

Be able to recognize when the odor is sour and strong versus rotten or putrid. If the fermentation smells nasty, not just sour, discard it.

Slimy vegetables

Some micro-organisms produce slime. It is often due to a too-warm environment or not enough salt. If the fermenting veggies are slimy, compost the vegetables.

Soft and Mushy Vegetables

Although there is nothing dangerous about mushy vegetables, they are unappetizing. Mushy vegetables usually occur because of too much heat or salt. Since it is not dangerous you could use mushy vegetables in a soup.

Crawly Things

When the vessel is left open, flies may lay eggs in the fermentation and worms will grow. I personally would compost the whole batch, but technically the eggs are only on the surface, so the top layer could be removed.

Pink

If your kraut turns pink and there are no pink vegetables in your mix, this is an indication the microorganisms are growing improperly. Again, discard the fermentation.

How to Prepare Different Types of Veggies

If you do a web search you will find there as many ways to make sauerkraut as there are people making it. Everyone has their opinion on what works best. The general rule of thumb is 2 Tablespoons of salt per gallon of kraut. It is always important to have the ingredients submerged in liquid, so if you find there is not enough liquid, add more water. Most recipes recommend an airtight environment so find a setup that works for you. If your kraut is bad you will know by the rotten smell and you won't want to eat it.

Vegetables Ferments

The most common fermented vegetable is cabbage. Cabbage has a long history as a food used as medicine to treat digestive disorders, arthritis, tumors, and wounds. More recently, the sulfur containing compounds in cabbage have been used as antioxidants and anti-tumor medicines (Cheung, 2010). There is also research that has identified cabbage as a powerful anti-inflammatory within the digestive tract (Cheney, 1949). Cabbage has many cousins such as Napa cabbage, Tat Soi, Bok Choy, and others, all with similar properties. The base of traditional kraut recipes is usually cabbage and onion, as onion is a good prebiotic food, which helps the proliferation of beneficial bacteria.

Salt initiates a process called lacto-fermentation. In lacto-fermentation lactic acid is produced by the beneficial bacteria *lactobacilli* as they break down the vegetables. The lacto in lacto-fermentation refers to these bacteria. Lactic acid acts as a preservative and inhibits bad bacteria, which would otherwise putrefy the food. As the lactobacilli break down the starches and sugars, they improve the bioavailability of certain nutrients, produce helpful enzymes, and synthesize antibiotic/anti-carcinogenic substances.

Sea Salt

Salt can benefit your ferments in a multitude of ways. Salt pulls the moisture out of the veggies, which inhibits the growth of harmful bacteria. The remaining salty solution provides the perfect environment for *Lactobacilli* strains to grow. In addition, other bacteria are inhibited by salt. Salt creates the environment for only the *Lactobacilli*—already present on the vegetables being used— to grow. It is possible to use too much salt and halt the culturing process completely by killing all available microorganisms. Salt is preferred in vegetables that taste better when crunchy, because it hardens the pectin in the cell walls.

Sauerkraut

- 1 medium cabbage cored and sliced
- 1 onion, sliced
- 1 Tablespoon caraway seeds
- 1 bunch fresh dill or 1 Tablespoon dry dill
- 1 Tablespoon non-iodized sea salt

1. Mix all ingredients in a bowl, mashing or kneading to release the juices.
2. Place all ingredients including the released juices in a hermetically sealed jar. Press down until submerged in water. If the juices don't rise over the cabbage, then use an appropriately shaped jar to press the cabbage down with the lid of the hermetically sealed jar. Clamp the hermetically sealed jar shut to keep oxygen out. Let sit for 2-4 weeks and then put it in the refrigerator for slower fermentation.

Appendix VI: The Lymphatic System

The lymphatic system is composed of vessels, nodes, and glands. The primary function of the lymphatic system is to remove wastes from cells, regulate the immune cells, and deliver energy to the cells. This process begins in the digestive system where the body absorbs fats and processes undigested proteins like gluten, pollutants, toxins, pesticides, and preservatives.[105]

The lymphatic system is considered part of the immune system because it protects the cells. The white blood cells in the lymph make up 80% of your immunity.[106] When the lymph gets congested and is not able to transport immune cells to their desired location, hypersensitivity reactions are common. Not being able to remove wastes from the bloodstream adversely impacts immunity.[107] If the lymph is moving, then the B and T lymphocytes (white blood cells) can identify and attack pathogens and invaders that may pose a threat. This happens in the GALT (Gut Associated Lymphatic Tissue) and in the lymph nodes.

Gut Associated Lymphatic Tissue

The highest concentration of lymph tissue is in the digestive system. Within the small intestine, lymphatic capillaries called lacteals absorb and transport dietary lipids and lipid-soluble vitamins into the liver. This slurry is called "chyle." From the liver it enters the bloodstream. When this process goes wrong, then undigested proteins—along with toxic fats, environmental pollutants, pesticides, and preservatives—congest the lymph affecting the microbiome and inhibiting digestion.[108,109]

The next place this congested lymph goes is the skin-associated lymphatic tissue (SALT) and then on to the MALT (mucous-associated lymphoid tissue, which lines all the mucus membranes of the body), BALT (bronchial-associated lymphoid tissue in the bronchi), NALT (nasal-associated lymphoid tissue), and LALT (larynx-associated lymphoid tissue).[110]

As you can see, most of our lymphoid tissue is strongly associated with the respiratory and digestive systems. In *Ayurveda*, the *Kapha Dosha* is associated with these systems. The *Kapha Dosha* has five subtypes that relate to each of the lymphoid tissue mentioned.

5 Types of Kapha and Associated Lymphatic Tissue		
Kledaka	Digestion, mucous, the root of all other *Kapha*'s	GALT
Avalambaka	Low back and lungs	BALT
Bodhaka	Taste, smell	LALT
Tarpaka	Senses, cough, nasal congestion, cerebral spinal fluid	NALT
Shleshaka	Joint pain, congestion	SALT

The *Kapha Dosha* is also associated with *Ojas*. *Ojas* is our vitality and the resistance our tissues have to disease. The lymphatic system is very resilient and under most circumstances can "process" all the undigested material it encounters. When it does this, the tissues of the digestive system and respiratory system act as a barrier to pathogens. Over time certain foods and behaviors can weaken the lymphatic system's ability to detoxify the body, which can lead to problems.

Common Contributors to Lymph Congestion

Lymph vessels also transport hormones, but certain hormones can congest the lymph. The biggest culprits are stress hormones. Hormones such as cortisol and adrenaline, when secreted in excess, can congest the lymphatic system through free radical damage and can alter the PH of the blood, making it more acidic.[111,112] Hormone imbalances because of excess stress are one of the primary ways the lymph can become congested. This leads to swelling, cellulite, and cold hands.

Because the digestive system is where you are exposed to many of the substances the lymphatic vessels must "filter," it can be another common contributor to congestion. If you eat too much, eat too many foods that are hard to digest, or eat foods with common food allergies, it can overwhelm the lymph and lead to problems.[113]

Air pollution is another big contributor to lymph congestion. It is estimated that over 4 billion pounds of environmental toxins are dumped into the environment, and the lymphatic tissue detoxifies this in the respiratory tract.[7] Some common symptoms of lymph congestion are:

- Breast swelling or soreness with each menstrual cycle
- Dry skin
- Mild rash or acne
- Hypersensitivity
- Mild headaches
- Elevated histamine and irritation due to common environmental allergens
- Occasional constipation, diarrhea, and/or mucus in the stool

The Brain's Lymphatic System

Until recently it was believed there were no lymph vessels in the brain. Now, however, researchers at the University of Virginia School of Medicine discovered the brain and central nervous system are drained by meningeal lymphatic vessels called glymphatics, indicating there is a strong link between the immune system and the brain.[113] As with the rest of the body, these lymph vessels act as drains and, when clogged, allowing for the accumulation of neurotoxins such as beta-amyloid plaque. This plaque has been indicated in numerous cognitive and memory concerns that are only now starting to be more fully understood.[114]

The glymphatics are related to mood disorders. In studies on mood disorders, it was found that having an autoimmune condition can increase the risk of future mood-related concerns by 45%.[115] This is a powerful relationship between the mood, brain, and immune system.[116] Congestion that starts in the digestive system or lungs will eventually affect the brain and lead to an increase in infection, inflammation, auto-immunity, and psychiatric concerns.[117] Supporting the lymphatic system has wide-ranging effects on the body and mind.

Ayurveda and the Lymphatic System

Ayurveda has a whole arm of study focused on lymph. It is called *rasayana*. *Rasa* primarily means lymph, but it's also associated with taste, emotion, juice, and many other things. According to *Ayurveda*, it is the lymph that governs the emotional and hunger responses. *Rasa* is also the foundational tissue for every other tissue in the body. That is why the skin reflects digestive health in *Ayurveda*. Eighty percent of what your skin looks like on the outside is determined by the function of the skin on the inside. While the outer skin protects, nourishes, and detoxifies the body, the inner skin does the same inside of the body.

If the outer skin is dry, wrinkled, inflamed, or anything else, then the lymph is not functioning properly which, in turn, is an indication the digestive system's elimination channels are clogged. The skin becomes a primary detoxification channel.

Please refer to the *Rasayana* section of this book for more information on specific foods and lifestyle practices. Another approach to supporting lymphatic function is *garshana*, dry skin brushing with silk gloves (See Appendix III). This additional information of the function of lymphatics is meant to inspire you to do those practices.

Appendix VII: Stomach and HCl

Digestion is the cornerstone of health in *Ayurveda*. Digestion begins in the mouth and the first stop is the stomach. Once enough work has taken place in the mouth, food is swallowed into the esophagus. Peristalsis, aided by gravity, moves the food down the esophagus and into the stomach. Within the stomach gastrin hormone begins to coordinate the entire dance of digestion. Hydrochloric acid (HCl) heats food and kills bacteria. Pepsin splits proteins into smaller amino acid molecules, and mucus protects the stomach lining. From the *Ayurvedic* perspective, this first stage of digestion is the *Kapha* stage of digestion. It spans the time from first noticing a feeling of hunger (ie: 10-15 minutes before eating) until 30 minutes after.

It used to be that conditions like gastroesophageal reflux disease and heartburn were associated with high stomach acid. Now we know that they are caused by low stomach acid which leads to an *H. pylori* infection. *H. pylori* is a bacterium that burrows into the lining of the stomach, suppressing *parietal cells* from releasing hydrochloric acid, the enzyme we use to digest proteins.[118] In addition to heartburn and burping this can lead to bad breath and difficulty digesting rich proteins.

A lack of hydrochloric acid in the stomach can lead to poor digestion and eventually more serious conditions like atherosclerosis, gastric carcinoma, and Hashimoto's thyroiditis. Acidity in the stomach neutralizes other pathogens in addition to *H. pylori*. It is important to maintain the right amount of stomach acid for gastrointestinal health.

The Low Stomach Acid Epidemic

Low stomach acid, or hypochlorhydria, is arguably the most common gastrointestinal condition in the US.[119] Most readers will likely have it at some point. Low stomach acid is the cause of most of the underlying digestive issues readers struggle with. This is because the typical American diet lacks vegetables and is composed of processed foods high in sugar. This diet can lead to:

- Cramping or bloating
- Lack of hunger upon waking
- Weak, cracked, or peeling fingernails
- Chronic fatigue[120]
- Adrenal fatigue
- Chronic candida
- Multiple food allergies
- Undigested food in stools
- Acne

All of this can be alleviated by increasing the amount of HCl in the stomach.[121] HCl makes your stomach more acidic which promotes adequate levels of other enzymes. If you go to your doctor with these symptoms, they will prescribe PPI medication (proton-pump inhibitor) like Prilosec, Nexium, Zantac, or Pepcid. This treatment may make you feel better, but it will cause a lot of problems down the road, such as heart and kidney disease. These medications were not designed to be used for more than six to eight weeks but are often taken for years.

If high stomach acid isn't the problem, then what is? Low stomach acid leads to an increase in intra-abdominal pressure which pushes against the lower esophageal sphincter reducing its ability to keep a tight seal. Once this tight seal has been compromised then it only takes a small amount of stomach acid in the esophagus to cause significant pain and burning. The esophageal sphincter can weaken over time causing damage to the esophagus. The problem is low stomach acid, not high stomach acid.

Restore Stomach Acid Production

It is vital to restore stomach acid production, especially if you have been tested positive for *H. pylori*. The first step is reducing stress and to stop taking acid suppressing drugs. After that you may want to kickstart your acid production by taking hydrochloric acid (HCl). In the short term it will help with improved nutrient absorption. Take HCl with pepsin; pepsin is the digestive enzyme mentioned earlier that breaks down protein. HCl is usually derived from beets and Pepsin from pigs. Betaine HCl and pepsin will help you digest proteins in the stomach leading to the following benefits:

1. Improved digestion and less energy expenditure on digestion
2. Improved synthesis of neurotransmitters
3. Fewer food allergies
4. Fewer cravings for food

This is not a long-term strategy, as taking these digestive enzymes will create dependency. Over time you will need to change your diet and lifestyle so it supports healthy digestion. Taking enzymes will kick start your digestion and move you in that direction.

Alternate Ways to Support Stomach Acid

It has been found that apple cider vinegar, lemon juice, and beets all contain betaine. This phytochemical can break down homocysteine which is an indicator of inflammation in the body. That is why I have included a lot of these ingredients throughout the program. Supporting healthy stomach acid production is a key to a healthy digestive system and long-term health and wellness.

References

Why me? Why Ayurveda?

1. Ceballos, Gerardo; Ehrlich, Paul R. (8 June 2018). "The misunderstood sixth mass extinction". Science. 360 (6393): 1080–1081.
2. Hollingsworth, Julia (June 11, 2019). "Almost 600 plant species have become extinct in the last 250 years". CNN. Retrieved January 14, 2020. The research—published Monday in *Nature, Ecology & Evolution* journal—found that 571 plant species have disappeared from the wild worldwide, and that plant extinction is occurring up to 500 times faster than the rate it would without human intervention.
3. Lawton, J. H.; May, R. M. (1995). "Extinction Rates". *Journal of Evolutionary Biology*. 9: 124–126. doi:10.1046/j.1420-9101.1996.t01-1-9010124.x

Why Do This Program?

4. Centers for Disease Control. *Fourth National Report on Human Exposure to Environmental Chemicals*. www.cdc.gov/exposurereport/pdf Fourth Report-Executive Summa pdf
5. United States Environmental Protection Agency, Toxics Release Inventory Program www.epa.gov/TRI
6. C. Pelletier P Imbeault, and A. Tremblay Energy Balance and Pollution by organo-chlorines and Polychlorinated Biphenyl obesity Reviews 4, no. 1 (2003) 17-24 A. Tremblay, C. Pelletier, E.
7. Environmental Working Group. Bisphenol A. www.ewg.org/chemindbisphenolAchemicals/
8. Environmental Gr Working Human Toxome Project, Mapping the Pollution in People. www. sites/humantoxome
9. Environmental Working Group. Pharmaceuticals pollute tapwater. ww node/ 6128
10. Panchakarma therapy greatly reduces the levels of 14 important 'lipophilic (i.e. fat-soluble) toxic and carcinogenic chemicals in the body.
11. Sharma HM, Nidich S, Sands D, Smith DE. Improvement in cardiovascular risk factors through Panchakarma purification procedures. Journal of Research and Education in Indian Medicine, 1993, XI: 4, 2-13.Nidich SI, Smith DE, Sands D, Sharma H. Nidich RJ, Barnes V, Jossang S. Effect of Maharishi Ayur-Ved karma purification program on speed of processing ability. Maharishi International University, Fairfield, Iowa, USA.
12. Schneider RH Cavanaugh KL, Kasture HS, Rothenberg S, Averbach R, Robinson D, Wallace RK. Health promotion with a traditional system of natural health care: Maharishi Ayur-Veda. Journal of Social Behavior and Personality, 1990, 53): 1-2

Some of the Results

13. Y Tache and S. Brunnhuber. From Hans Selves discovery of biological stress to the identification of corticotropin-releasing factor signaling pathways: implication in stress-related functional bowel diseases.

14. Sharma HM, Nidich S, Sands D, Smith DE. Improvement in cardiovascular risk factors through Panchakarma purification procedures. *Journal of Research and Education in Indian Medicine*, 1993, XI: 4, 2-13.
15. Wilders-Truschnig, M., et al. 2007 IgE antibodies against food antigens are correlated with inflammation and intima media thickness in obese juveniles. Exp Clin Endocrinal Diabetes 116 (4):241-45
16. Panchakarma therapy greatly reduces the levels of 14 important 'lipophilic (i.e. fat-soluble) toxic and carcinogenic chemicals in the body.
17. Susan J. Torres and Caryl A Nowson. Relationship between stress, eating behavior and obesity. Nutrition 2007:23:887-894
18. Nidich SI, Smith DE, Sands D, Sharma H. Nidich RJ, Barnes V, Jossang S. Effect of Maharishi Ayur-Ved karma purification program on speed of processing ability. Maharishi International University, Fairfield, Iowa, USA.

History of Ayurveda

19. Subbarayappa BV. A perspective. Medicine and Life Sciences in India. In: Subbarayappa BV, editor. New Delhi: Centre for Studies in Civilizations; 2001. pp. 1–38. Chattopadhyay DP, general editor. *History of Science, Philosophy and Culture in Indian Civilization; Part 2.* Vol. IV)
20. Mazars G. Indian medicine across the centuries. A Concise Introduction to Indian Medicine (La médecine indienne). Gopalan TK, translator. Ch. 1. In: Wujastyk D, Zysk KG, editors. Delhi: Motilal Banarsidass Publishers Private Limited; 2006. pp. 1–24. *Indian Medical Tradition; Vol. VIII*
21. Gopinath BG. Foundational ideas of *Ayurveda*. Medicine and Life Sciences in India. In: Subbarayappa BV, Chattopadhyay DP, editors. New Delhi: Centre for Studies in Civilizations; 2001. pp. 59–107. *History of Science, Philosophy and Culture in Indian Civilization; Part 2.* Vol. IV.

Dietary Recommendations for the Spring (*Kapha*) Season

22. T Colin Campbell and Thomas M. Campbell, *The China Study* (BenBella Books Dallas, 2006)
23. E. T Poehlman, P J. Arciero, C. L. Melby, and S. F. Badylak, "Resting Metabolic Rate and Postprandial Thermogenesis in Vegetarians and Nonvegetarians *American Journal of Clinical Nutrition 48*, no. 2 (1988): 209-13
24. S. E. McCann, J. L. Fredenheim, J. R. Marshall, and S. Graham, "Risk of Human ovarian Cancer Is Related to Dietary Intake of Selected Nutrients, Phytochemicals and Food Groups *Journal of Nutrition 133*, no. 6 (2003): 1937-42
25. K. A. Steinmetz and J. D. Potter "Vegetables, Fruit and Cancer Prevention: A Review 1996 *Journal of the American Dietetic Association 96*, no. 10 1027-39
26. Y Papikolaou and V. L. Fulgoni, "Bean Consumption Is Associated with Greater Nutrient intake, Reduced Systolic Blood Pressure, Lower Body Weight, and a smaller waist Circumference in Adults": Results from the National Health and Nutrition Examination Survey 999-2002, Journal of the American College of Nutrition 27, no. 5 (2008): 569-76

27. F.B. Hu, J E. Manson, and W.C. Willett, "Types of Dietary Fat and Risk of Coronary Disease: A Critical Review," Journal of the American College of Nutrition 20, no (2001): 5-19

28. Leray C. 2010. Cyberlipid Center.: Resource site for lipid studies. Available from: http://www.cyberlipid.org/cyberlip/home0001.htm

29. Femke Lutgendorff Louis M. A. Akkermans, and Johan D. Soderholm The role of microbiota and probiotics in stress-induced gastro-intestinal damage. Curr Mol Med 2008;8:282-298

30. Tapsell LC, Hemphill I, Cobiac L, Patch CS, Sullivan DR, Fenech M, Roodenrys S, Keogh JB, Clifton PM, Williams PG, Fazio VA, Inge KE. 2006. Health benefits of herbs and spices: the past, the present, the future. Med.J Aust. 185(4 Suppl):S4-24

31. Yolanda Gonzalez et al. High glucose concentrations induce TNF-alpha production through the down-regulation of CD33 in primary human monocytes. BMC Immunology 2012; 13:19, DOI: 10.1186/1471 -2172-13-19 6.

32. Angel Gil-Izquierdo, Maria I. Gil, and Federico Ferreres, "Effect of Processing Techniques at Industrial Scale on Orange Juice Antioxidant and Beneficial Health Compounds," *Journal of Agricultural and Food Chemistry 50*, no. 18 (2002): 5107-14

33. Deborah Rothman, Pamela DeLuca, and Robert B. Zurier. Botanical lipids: effects on inflammation, immune responses and rheumatoid arthritis. Semi Arthritis Rheu 1995 Oct 25(2):87-96

34. Anna Sapone et al. Spectrum of gluten-related disorders: consensus on new nomenclature and classification. BMC Medicine 2012; 10:13 2.

35. Paimela al. Gliadin immune reactivity in patient with rheumatoid arthritis. Clin et Exp Rheumatol 1995 Sep-Oct; 13(5):603-607 4.

36. Amy C. Brown. Gluten sensitivity: problems of an emerging condition separate f celiac disease. Expert Rev Gastroenterol Hepatol 2012;6(1):43-55 5.

Recommended Appliances

37. Leaching of aluminum from aluminum dishes and packages. Liukkonen-Lilja H, Piepponen S. Food Addit Contam. 1992 May-Jun;9(3):213-23. PMID: 1397396

38. Hesperidin and Silibinin Ameliorate Aluminum-Induced Neurotoxicity: Modulation of Antioxidants and Inflammatory Cytokines Level in Mice Hippocampus. Jangra A, Kasbe P, Pandey SN, Dwivedi S, Gurjar SS, Kwatra M, Mishra M, Venu AK, Sulakhiya K, Gogoi R, Sarma N, Bezbaruah BK, Lahkar M. Biol Trace Elem Res. 2015 May 28. [Epub ahead of print]PMID: 26018497

39. https://www.scienceofcooking.com/science_of_pressure_cooking.htm

40. http://www.discoverpressurecooking.com/use.html

Recommended Brands

41. https://pubs.acs.org/doi/abs/10.1021/acs.est.9b02540

Herbal Guidelines for the Spring Ayurvedic Cleanse

42. Baskaran K et al. Antidiabetic effect of leaf extract from Gymnema sylvestre a in noninsulin-dependent diabetes mellitus patients. J Ethnopharmacol1990, 30:295

43. Shanmugasundaram ER. et al. Use of Gynmema sylvestre leaf extract in the control of blood glucose in insulin-dependent diabetes mellitus. J Ethnopharmacol1990, 30:281

44. Murunikkara V1, Rasool MK1.Trikatu, a herbal compound mitigates the biochemical and immunological complications in adjuvant-induced arthritic rats. https://www.ncbi.nlm.nih.gov/pubmed/25546349

45. Roy S1, Yasmin S2, Ghosh S2, Bhattacharya S2, Banerjee D2.Anti-Infective Metabolites of a Newly Isolated Bacillus thuringiensis KL1 Associated with Kalmegh (Andrographis paniculata Nees.), a Traditional Medicinal Herb.

46. Peterson CT1,2, Denniston K3, Chopra D1,2.Therapeutic Uses of Triphala in Ayurvedic Medicine. https://www.ncbi.nlm.nih.gov/pubmed/28696777

47. Wang L, Sun Y, Antidepressant Effects and Mechanisms of the Total Iridoids of Valeriana jatamansi on the Brain-Gut Axis. https://www.ncbi.nlm.nih.gov/pubmed/31801162

48. Radhika C, Kumar GV, Mihirjan K. A randomized controlled clinical trial to assess the efficacy of Nasya in reducing the signs and symptoms of cervical spondylosis. https://www.ncbi.nlm.nih.gov/pubmed/23049188

49. Rao GM, Rao CV. Hepatoprotective effects of rubiadin, a major constituent of Rubia cordifolia Linn. http://www.ncbi.nlm.nih.gov/pubmed/16213120

50. Tripathi YB, Singh AV. Role of Rubia cordifolia Linn. in radiation protection. http://www.ncbi.nlm.nih.gov/pubmed/17821858

51. Shweta lodi, Veena Sharma, The protective effect of Rubia cordifolia against lead nitrate-induced immune response impairment and kidney oxidative damage

52. Le XT, Pham HT. Bacopa monnieri ameliorates memory deficits in olfactory bulbectomized mice: possible involvement of glutamatergic and cholinergic systems.

53. Md Mizanur Rahman, Mohammad Nazmul Alam, Cardamom powder supplementation prevents obesity, improves glucose intolerance, inflammation and oxidative stress in liver of high carbohydrate high fat diet induced obese rats https://www.ncbi.nlm.nih.gov/pmc/articles/PMC5557534

54. Kalpana Plate, K.Srinivasan Ph.D. Stimulatory influence of select spices on bile secretion in rats. https://www.sciencedirect.com/science/article/pii/S0271531700800305

55. Kashmira J. Gohil, Jagruti A. Patel, Pharmacological Review on Centella asiatica: A Potential Herbal Cure-all http://www.ncbi.nlm.nih.gov/pmc/articles/PMC3116297/

56. Kashmira J. Gohil, Jagruti A. Patel, Pharmacological Review on Centella asiatica: A Potential Herbal Cure-all http://www.ncbi.nlm.nih.gov/pmc/articles/PMC3116297/

Digestive Tea to Improve Hydration

57. Barry M. Popkin, Water, Hydration and Health https://www.ncbi.nlm.nih.gov/pmc/articles/PMC2908954

Day 1-3 Preparation Phase

58. Kohli DR, Lee JZ-E, Koch TR, Talavera F, Anand BS, Greenwald D, et al. Achlorhydria Clinical Presentation. Medscape. http://emedicine.medscape.com/article/170066-clinical#b5. Updated July 15, 2016. Accessed May 3, 2018.

59. R. Ramakrishna Rao, Kalpana Platel. In vitro influence of spices and spice-active principles on digestive enzymes of rat pancreas and small intestine. http://onlinelibrary.wiley.com/doi/10.1002/food.200390091/abstract

60. https://www.researchgate.net/publication/320402962_Chemical_Composition_and_Biological_Activities_of_Lemon_Citrus_limon_Leaf_Essential_Oil https://www.ncbi.nlm.nih.gov/pmc/articles/PMC1350392/

61. ^ Reicks MM, Crankshaw D. Effects of D-limonene on hepatic microsomal monooxygenase activity and paracetamol-induced glutathione depletion in mouse. *Xenobiotica*. (1993)

62. Fukuchi Y, et al. Lemon Polyphenols Suppress Diet-induced Obesity by Up-Regulation of mRNA Levels of the Enzymes Involved in beta-Oxidation in Mouse White Adipose Tissue. *J Clin Biochem Nutr*. (2008)

63. Penniston KL, et al. Quantitative assessment of citric acid in lemon juice, lime juice, and commercially-available fruit juice products. *J Endourol*. (2008)

Day 4-7 Main Cleanse Step One

64. Bouderbala H, Anti-obesogenic effect of apple cider vinegar in rats subjected to a high fat diet]. https://www.ncbi.nlm.nih.gov/pubmed/27209492

65. Y Sun, T Yang, L Mao, and F Zhang Sulforaphane Protects against Brain Diseases: Roles of Cytoprotective Enzymes. Cerebrovasc Dis Stroke. 2017; 4(1): 1054.

66. Runping Yang, Qiang Zhou, Chunmiao Wen, Jian Hu, Hengjin Li, Ming Zhao, Hua Zhao. Mustard Seed (Sinapis Alba Linn) Attenuates Imiquimod-Induced Psoriasiform Inflammation of BALB/c Mice. J Dermatol. 2013 Jul;40(7):543-52. doi: 10.1111/1346-8138.12119. Epub 2013 May 19. https://pubmed.ncbi.nlm.nih.gov/23682616/?i=3&from=/22159228/related

67. Tiku AB, Abraham SK, Kale RK. Protective effect of the cruciferous vegetable mustard leaf (Brassica campestris) against in vivo chromosomal damage and oxidative stress induced by gamma-radiation and genotoxic chemicals. Environ Mol Mutagen. 2008 Jun;49(5):335-42. doi: 10.1002/em.20383. https://www.ncbi.nlm.nih.gov/pubmed/18418865

Day 8-10: Main Phase: Step Two

68. Hatori, M., Vollmers, C., Zarrinpar, A., DiTacchio, L., Bushong, E. A., Gill, S., ... & Ellisman, M. H. (2012). Time-restricted feeding without reducing caloric intake prevents metabolic diseases in mice fed a high-fat diet. *Cell metabolism*, 15(6), 848-860.

69. Chaix, A., Zarrinpar, A., Miu, P., & Panda, S. (2014). Time-restricted feeding is a preventative and therapeutic intervention against diverse nutritional challenges. *Cell metabolism*, 20(6), 991-1005.

70. Jagdish Singh, A.K. Upadhyay, A. Bahadur, B. Singh, K.P. Singh, Mathura Rai. Antioxidant phytochemicals in cabbage (Brassica oleracea L. var. capitata). https://www.sciencedirect.com/science/article/abs/pii/S0304423806000483
71. Ock Kyoung Chun, Nancy Smith, Amber Sakagawa & Chang Yong Lee. Antioxidant properties of raw and processed cabbages. https://www.tandfonline.com/doi/abs/10.1080/09637480410001725148
72. Valli Kannan, Extraction of Bioactive Compounds from Whole Red Cabbage and Beetroot using Pulsed Electric Fields and Evaluation of their Functionality. https://digitalcommons.unl.edu/foodscidiss/11/
73. Meredith Petrie, W. Jack Rejeski, Swati Basu, Paul J Laurienti, Anthony P Marsh, James L Norris, Daniel B Kim-Shapiro, Jonathan H Burdette. Beet Root Juice: An Ergogenic Aid for Exercise and the Aging Brain. The Journals of Gerontology: Series A, Volume 72, Issue 9, September 2017, Pages 1284–1289, https://doi.org/10.1093/gerona/glw219
74. Yikyung Park, Amy F. Subar, Albert Hollenbeck, and Arthur Schatzkin, MD. Dietary fiber intake and mortality in the NIH-AARP Diet and Health Study. Arch Intern Med. 2011 Jun 27; 171(12): 1061–1068. https://www.ncbi.nlm.nih.gov/pmc/articles/PMC3513325/

Day 11-14 Integration Phase

75. Christian LM, Galley JD, Gut microbiome composition is associated with temperament during early childhood. http://www.ncbi.nlm.nih.gov/pubmed/25449582
76. Elena Biagi, Marco Candela, Ageing of the human meta organism: the microbial counterpart http://www.ncbi.nlm.nih.gov/pmc/articles/PMC3260362/

Appendix II: Fermented Cereals and Legumes

77. Cordain L, Toohey L, Smith MJ, Hickey MS. .Modulation of immune function by dietary lectins in rheumatoid arthritis. https://www.ncbi.nlm.nih.gov/pubmed/10884708
78. Vijayakumari K, Siddhuraju P, Janardhanan K. Effect of different post-harvest treatments on antinutritional factors in seeds of the tribal pulse, Mucuna pruriens https://www.ncbi.nlm.nih.gov/pubmed/8735780
79. Liang J, Han BZ, Nout MJR, Hamer RJ. 2008. Effects of soaking, germination and fermentation on phytic acid, total and in vitro soluble zinc in brown rice. *Food Chemistry.* 110(4): 821-828
80. Sharma A, Sehgal s. 1992. Effect of processing and cooking on the antinutritional factors of faba bean (Vicia faba). *Food Chemistry.* 43(5):383-385

Appendix III: Dry Skin Brushing with Silk Gloves – Garshana

81. Katie Rodan, MD, Kathy Fields, MD, George Majewski, and Timothy Falla, PhD. Skincare Bootcamp: The Evolving Role of Skincare. Plast Reconstr Surg Glob Open. 2016 Dec; 4(12 Suppl): e1152.
82. V. Bayrakci Tunay. Effects of mechanical massage, manual lymphatic drainage and connective tissue manipulation techniques on fat mass in women with cellulite. First published:07 January 2010. https://doi.org/10.1111/j.1468-3083.2009.03355.x

83. Dr Cyndi Gilbert N. Dry Skin Brushing [Internet]. Dr Cyndi Gilbert ND. 2012 [cited 2 June 2016]. Available from: http://www.cyndigilbert.ca/dry-skin-brushing/
84. Janda K, Tomikowska A. Cellulite—causes, prevention, treatment. [Article in Polish] Ann Acad Med Stetin. 2014;60(1):29-38.
85. Cellulite. (2016). nchmd.org/education/mayo-health-library/details/CON-20212580
86. Cellulite treatments: What really works? (2017). aad.org/public/diseases/cosmetic-treatments/cellulite-treatments
87. Giampietro L Vairo, Sayers John Miller, Nicole M McBrier, and William E Buckley. Systematic Review of Efficacy for Manual Lymphatic Drainage Techniques in Sports Medicine and Rehabilitation: An Evidence-Based Practice Approach. J Man Manip Ther. 2009; 17(3): e80–e89. doi: 10.1179/jmt.2009.17.3.80E

Appendix IV: Making Sprouts

88. Egner PA, Chen JG, Zarth AT, et al. Rapid and sustainable detoxication of airborne pollutants by broccoli sprout beverage: results of a randomized clinical trial in China. *Cancer Prev Res (Phila)*. 2014;7(8):813–823. doi:10.1158/1940-6207.CAPR-14-0103
89. Nagata N, Xu L, Kohno S, Ushida Y, Aoki Y, Umeda R, Fuke N, Zhuge F, Ni Y, Nagashimada M, Takahashi C, Suganuma H, Kaneko S, Ota T. Glucoraphanin Ameliorates Obesity and Insulin Resistance Through Adipose Tissue Browning and Reduction of Metabolic Endotoxemia in Mice. Diabetes. 2017 May;66(5):1222-1236. doi: 10.2337/db16-0662. Epub 2017 Feb 16.
90. Singh K, Connors SL, Macklin EA, Smith KD, Fahey JW, Talalay P, Zimmerman AW Sulforaphane treatment of autism spectrum disorder (ASD). Proc Natl Acad Sci U S A. 2014 Oct 28;111(43):15550-5. doi: 10.1073/pnas.1416940111. Epub 2014 Oct 13.
91. Bent, S., Lawton, B., Warren, T. *et al.* Identification of urinary metabolites that correlate with clinical improvements in children with autism treated with sulforaphane from broccoli. *Molecular Autism* **9,** 35 (2018). https://doi.org/10.1186/s13229-018-0218-4
92. Benedict AL, Mountney A, Hurtado A, et al. Neuroprotective effects of sulforaphane after contusive spinal cord injury. *J Neurotrauma*. 2012;29(16):2576–2586. doi:10.1089/neu.2012.2474
93. Hong Y, Yan W, Chen S, Sun CR, Zhang JM. The role of Nrf2 signaling in the regulation of antioxidants and detoxifying enzymes after traumatic brain injury in rats and mice. Acta Pharmacol Sin. 2010 Nov;31(11):1421-30. doi: 10.1038/aps.2010.101. Epub 2010 Oct 18.
94. Dash PK, Zhao J, Orsi SA, Zhang M, Moore AN. Sulforaphane improves cognitive function administered following traumatic brain injury. Neurosci Lett. 2009 Aug 28;460(2):103-7. doi: 10.1016/j.neulet.2009.04.028. Epub 2009 Apr 15.
95. Morroni F, Tarozzi A, Sita G, Bolondi C, Zolezzi Moraga JM, Cantelli-Forti G, Hrelia P. Neuroprotective effect of sulforaphane in 6-hydroxydopamine-lesioned mouse model of Parkinson's disease. Neurotoxicology. 2013 May;36:63-71. doi: 10.1016/j.neuro.2013.03.004. Epub 2013 Mar 18.
96. Martín-de-Saavedra MD, Budni J, Cunha MP, Gómez-Rangel V, Lorrio S, Del Barrio L, Lastres-Becker I, Parada E, Tordera RM, Rodrigues AL, Cuadrado A, López MG. Nrf2 participates in depressive disorders through an anti-inflammatory

mechanism. Psychoneuroendocrinology. 2013 Oct;38(10):2010-22. doi: 10.1016/j.psyneuen.2013.03.020. Epub 2013 Apr 23. PubMed PMID: 23623252.

97. Wu S, Gao Q, Zhao P, Gao Y, Xi Y, Wang X, Liang Y, Shi H, Ma Y. Sulforaphane produces antidepressant- and anxiolytic-like effects in adult mice. Behav Brain Res. 2016 Mar 15;301:55-62. doi: 10.1016/j.bbr.2015.12.030. Epub 2015 Dec 22.

98. Riedl MA, Saxon A, Diaz-Sanchez D. Oral sulforaphane increases Phase II antioxidant enzymes in the human upper airway. *Clin Immunol.* 2009;130(3):244-251. doi:10.1016/j.clim.2008.10.007

99. Kikuchi M, Ushida Y, Shiozawa H, et al. Sulforaphane-rich broccoli sprout extract improves hepatic abnormalities in male subjects. *World J Gastroenterol.* 2015;21(43):12457-12467. doi:10.3748/wjg.v21.i43.12457

100. Pal S, Konkimalla VB. Data on sulforaphane treatment mediated suppression of autoreactive, inflammatory M1 macrophages. Data Brief. 2016 Apr 25;7:1560-4. doi: 10.1016/j.dib.2016.03.105. eCollection 2016 Jun.

101. Kim HJ, Barajas B, Wang M, Nel AE. Nrf2 activation by sulforaphane restores the age-related decrease of T(H)1 immunity: role of dendritic cells. *J Allergy Clin Immunol.* 2008;121(5):1255-1261.e7. doi:10.1016/j.jaci.2008.01.016

102. Fahey JW, Haristoy X, Dolan PM, et al. Sulforaphane inhibits extracellular, intracellular, and antibiotic-resistant strains of Helicobacter pylori and prevents benzo[a]pyrene-induced stomach tumors. *Proc Natl Acad Sci U S A.* 2002;99(11):7610-7615. doi:10.1073/pnas.112203099

103. Romeo, L.; Iori, R.; Rollin, P.; Bramanti, P.; Mazzon, E. Isothiocyanates: An Overview of Their Antimicrobial Activity against Human Infections. *Molecules* 2018, 23, 624.

104. Müller L, Meyer M, Bauer RN, et al. Effect of Broccoli Sprouts and Live Attenuated Influenza Virus on Peripheral Blood Natural Killer Cells: A Randomized, Double-Blind Study. *PLoS One.* 2016;11(1):e0147742. Published 2016 Jan 28. doi:10.1371/journal.pone.0147742

Appendix VI: The Lymphatic System

105. J. Brandon Dixon. Lymphatic Lipid Transport: Sewer or Subway? Trends Endocrinol Metab. 2010 Aug; 21(8): 480–487. Published online 2010 Jun 11. doi: 10.1016/j.tem.2010.04.003

106. Iurii Koboziev, Fridrik Karlsson, and Matthew B. Grisham. Gut-associated lymphoid tissue, T cell trafficking, and chronic intestinal inflammation. Ann N Y Acad Sci. 2010 Oct; 1207(Suppl 1): E86–E93. doi: 10.1111/j.1749-6632.2010.05711.x

107. Pimpinelli N1, Santucci M. The skin-associated lymphoid tissue-related B-cell lymphomas. Semin Cutan Med Surg. 2000 Jun;19(2):124-9. http://www.ncbi.nlm.nih.gov/pubmed/10892714

108. V. Lobo, A. Patil, A. Phatak, and N. Chandra. Free radicals, antioxidants and functional foods: Impact on human health. Pharmacogn Rev. 2010 Jul-Dec; 4(8): 118-126. doi: 10.4103/0973-7847.70902

109. Sanjukta Chakraborty,1 Scott Zawieja,1 Wei Wang, David C. Zawieja,1 and Mariappan Muthuchamy, Lymphatic system acts as a vital link between metabolic syndrome and inflammation. Ann N Y Acad Sci. 2010 Oct; 1207(Suppl 1): E94-102. doi: 10.1111/j.1749-6632.2010.05752.x

110. Bharat B. Aggarwal, Sahdeo Prasad, Simone Reuter, Ramaswamy Kannappan, Vivek R. Yadev, Byoungduck Park, Ji Hye Kim, Subash C. Gupta, Kanokkarn Phromnoi, Chitra Sundaram, Seema Prasad, Madan M. Chaturvedi, and Bokyung Sung. Identification of Novel Anti-inflammatory Agents from Ayurvedic Medicine for Prevention of Chronic Diseases "Reverse Pharmacology" and "Bedside to Bench" Approach. Curr Drug Targets. 2011 Oct 1; 12(11): 1595–1653.

111. http://www.epa.gov/sites/production/files/2016-01/documents/3_tri_na_releases_of_chemicals_ry2014.pdf

112. http://www.nature.com/nature/journal/vaop/ncurrent/full/nature14432.html

113. Bloom GS Amyloid-β and tau: the trigger and bullet in Alzheimer disease pathogenesis. JAMA Neurol. 2014 Apr;71(4):505-8. doi: 10.1001/jamaneurol.2013.5847. http://www.ncbi.nlm.nih.gov/pubmed/24493463

114. Hurtado DE1, Molina-Porcel L, Iba M, Aboagye AK, Paul SM, Trojanowski JQ, Lee VM. A{beta} accelerates the spatiotemporal progression of tau pathology and augments tau amyloidosis in an Alzheimer mouse model. Am J Pathol. 2010 Oct;177(4):1977-88. doi: 10.2353/ajpath.2010.100346. Epub 2010 Aug 27. http://www.ncbi.nlm.nih.gov/pubmed/20802182

115. Takata K1, Kitamura Y, Taniguchi T. [Pathological changes induced by amyloid-β in Alzheimer's disease]. Yakugaku Zasshi. 2011 Jan;131(1):3-11.

116. http://www.nature.com/nature/journal/v523/n7560/full/nature14432.html

117. Michael E. Benros; Berit L. Waltoft; Merete Nordentoft; et al. Autoimmune Diseases and Severe Infections as Risk Factors for Mood Disorders A Nationwide Study. August 2013

Appendix VII: Stomach and HCl References

118. Aghili R, Jafarzadeh F, Bhorbani R, Khamseh ME, Salami MA, Malek M. *The association of Helicobacter pylori infection with Hashimoto's thyroiditis*. Acta Med Iran. 2013;51(5):293-296.

119. Kohli DR, Lee JZ-E, Koch TR, Talavera F, Anand BS, Greenwald D, et al. Achlorhydria Clinical Presentation. Medscape. http://emedicine.medscape.com/article/170066-clinical#b5. Updated July 15, 2016. Accessed May 3, 2018.

120. Betesh AL, Santa Ana CA, Cole JA, Fordtran JS. Is achlorhydria a cause of iron deficiency anemia? *Am J Clin Nutr*. 2015;102(1):9-19.

121. Betaine HCl with Pepsin. Supplement Information. Pure Encapsulations. https://www.purerxo.com/thyroidpharmacist/rxo/products/product_details.asp?ProductsID=929. Accessed April 2020.

Index

Agni, 29
    Balanced, 29
    Hot, 29
    Sluggish, 30
    Irregular, 31

Ayurveda, 19
    Elements, 22
    Constitution Types, 24
    Vata, 24
    Pitta, 24
    Kapha, 24

Cleansing, 13
    Results, 15

Cookware
    Fermenting Grains, 175
    Pressure Cooking, 175

Digestion
    Digestive Types, 29
    Six Tastes, 55

Doshas, See Constitution Types

Diet
    Spring Diet, 57
    Calorie Restriction, 124

Four Phases
    Day 1–3: Preparation Phase, 83
    Day 4–7: Main Cleanse
        Step One, 101
    Day 8–10: Main Cleanse
        Step Two, 123
    Day 11–14:
        Integration Phase, 141

Herbal Guidelines, 69

Lifestyle Guidelines, 73
    Sleep, 74
    Garshana, 178

Ojas, 25

Rasayana, 162

Shopping Lists
    Preparation Phase, 99
    Main Cleanse Step One, 121
    Main Cleanse Step Two, 139
    Integration Phase, 156
    Pantry Shopping List, 64

Tongue Monitoring, 75

Recipes Index

Day 1-3: Preparation Phase
Lemon Berry Cooli, **90**
Spring Spice Churna, **91**
Warm Zingy Green Smoothie, **92**
Savory Millet Breakfast Porridge, **93**
Millet Burgers, **94**
Detox Tabbouleh, **95**
Green Soup, **96**
Beet Borsht, **98**

Day 4-7: Main Cleanse Step One
Apple Cider Vinegar Elixir, **108**
Broccoli Sprouts, **109**
Simple *Kichari*, **112**
Quinoa *Kichari*, **114**
Kapha Reducing *Kichari*, **115**
Rosemary and Basil *Kichari*, **116**
Spicy *Kichari*, **117**
Coconut and Shitake *Kichari*, **118**
East Indian *Kichari*, **119**
Kichari Dumplings, **120**

Day 8-10: Main Cleanse Step Two
Spring Balancing Bowl, **130**
Cauliflower Rice and Tahini Veggies, **132**
Wild Rice and Beet Salad, **133**
Mung Bean Carrot Burgers, **135**
Raw Cauliflower Sunflower Cheese, **136**
Spring Salad with Kraut, **137**
Celery and Avocado Snack, **138**

Day 11-14: Integration Phase
Kapha Kraut, **148**
Green Smoothie, **149**
Apple Arugula Smoothie, **149**
Buckwheat Crepes with Ginger Chutney, **150**
Spring Salad with Kraut, **152**
Amaranth Bowl with Salsa Verde, **153**
Cauliflower and Pistachio Salad, **154**
Mustard Marinated Kale with Asparagus, **155**

Acknowledgements

I want to acknowledge all those who made this book a reality. My editor, Anneliese Kamola who helped me find my voice and express it with utmost clarity and brevity. ElfElm Publishing whose layout work made the book look it's best. And most of all to my patients without whom this book would not be possible. From the work we have done together as a team, you have shown me the remarkable healing power we all hold within ourselves. Thank you!

About The Author

Dr. Noah Volz is an *Ayurvedic* doctor, chiropractor, and yoga teacher. He has been sharing his gifts with the world since 2002 when he first started learning about *Ayurveda* and fell in love. He has taught countless classes across the US and has a deep passion for sharing the wisdom of *Ayurveda* with the world.

Other books by Dr. Volz include:

- *Blissful Belly: A 16-day Program for Super-Charging your Digestion using the Art and Science of Ayurveda*
- *New Year Re-Solution: A 14-Day Ayurvedic Program to Lose Weight and Feel Your Best*
- *14 Day Winter Home Cleanse: A Seasonal Ayurvedic Program to Shed Weight, Reduce Inflammation, and Reboot Your Metabolism*

You can learn more about Dr. Volz at www.rhythmofhealing.com

www.ingramcontent.com/pod-product-compliance
Lightning Source LLC
Chambersburg PA
CBHW061141010526
44118CB00026B/2839